Introduction

I was not born in New Orleans, but it has been my spiritual home from the first day I arrived. I was born in Omaha, Nebraska, in 1920. I lived in my grandmother's house and was surrounded by three women who looked after me very well. Jazz was certainly a new fad in Omaha, and I probably heard my first sound of it when I was about four years old. My aunt gave piano lessons, and my older cousin Meredith was always complimented on her singing ability. One of the first songs I remember them playing and singing was "Bye Bye Blackbird."

Al Rose was one of the great promoters of jazz in New Orleans and many other cities. Whenever he met someone for the first time, his special routine was to ask the names of the earliest songs that person could remember. With his expertise he could probably pinpoint the person's age immediately. I thought it was a great way to begin a new friendship. The first piece of jazz that I was enamored with was "Yes Sir, That's My Baby, – No Sir, I Don't Mean Maybe." Even though I was still too small to play the piano I could play those first two lines with two fingers on two keys; I thought I was a great success.

My aunt also played "The Darktown Strutters Ball" and that was about the limit of my knowledge, but I really liked the jazz sound. However, I was never cut out to be a musician. When I hit high school, the music of swing and sock hops in the gym temporarily passed up the exuberant sound of jazz.

I went on to graduate from Grinnell College in Iowa. Believe it or not, we were able to get really good bands from Chicago to play for our dances. The music was still predominantly swing, but we did hear a touch of jazz. It now seems strange to realize such well known bands as Tommy Dorsey, Bob Crosby, Woody Herman, and Kay Kayser would come to a small college, but Grinnell was one of the "Little Ivy League" schools, it possessed a solid financial reputation, and was located fairly close to Chicago. Those were the depression years and musicians were glad to get any work. Plus, they knew the college would pay them. One of those bands hit town during a big snow storm. We were safe enough on campus, but the band members couldn't get past the snow drifts in the streets that night, so they had to stay over.

I was sitting cross-legged on the floor on December 7, 1941, "watching" the radio. (We didn't just listen to the radio in those days. We tended to watch the radio as if an image would appear, . . . and it did appear in our minds.) We suddenly got the news that Pearl Harbor had been attacked by Japan. The whole world changed. Many of the boys finished that semester and then enlisted in the armed services. Bugle music of the jazz days once again entered the scene. In spite of the popularity of swing time, jazz was still hanging in there.

I received a teaching assistantship at Tulane University in New Orleans and also spent two summers doing botanical drawings at Northwestern University in Evanston, near Chicago. Now I had two reintroductions to jazz: New Orleans and Chicago. As graduate students at Tulane, we usually banded together in groups of eight or ten and hit the French Quarter (called the Vieux Carre by the old French people) on Saturday nights. There were many places to eat and a plethora of antique shops, so we also window shopped. The Napoleon House, a favorite college student hangout, played operas and classical music on the jukebox. That was a pleasant surprise, but when we went forth into the streets again, the sound of jazz burst from the nightclubs, pervading the Quarter. The sound was so exhilarating that it sent out a "feel good" sensation to everyone who heard it. No one could be depressed in such an atmosphere. I fell in love with New Orleans and explored every avenue of entertainment, including the parks, the lake front, and the big Mississippi River. I understood why they wrote so much music about the river.

While I was in Chicago during the summers, I heard jazz there as well. One night we visited a bar where Gene Krupa and his band were playing. There was a long narrow stage along the wall behind the bar and Krupa really threw all of his energy into his drums. I had never heard anyone play drums like that.

Shortly, I was back in New Orleans again listening to the sound of basic jazz. We often went to The Famous Door on Bourbon Street to hear the Dukes of Dixieland. We hit the Paddock, also on Bourbon, a few times when Sharkey Bonano was playing. It was a small place decorated with pictures of horses and horse-shoes hanging on the wall behind the bar.

Introduction
...continued

Later on, Crazy Shirley's was a place where one could hear the old Dixieland Jazz. There were many other places, but we did not have time or money to get around to all of them. For awhile, Sharkey was quite popular at college dances. He apparently had a personality change of some sort and began to get angry and fire people from his band when they offended him. One night he fired the whole band. As a result, no one wanted to work with him and he could no longer put a band together.

Early in the 1960s Allen and Sandra Jaffe, with the backing and support of Larry Borenstein, opened Preservation Hall to showcase the truly old-time jazz musicians. It soon became a favorite place for all who went to the Quarter. I called it "purist jazz." When they played, you could feel it in your bones. You have to be in New Orleans and the Hall to appreciate what a wonderful thing the Jaffes and Borenstein did; they really helped preserve the sound of traditional jazz.

I only knew that for me, jazz sounded better in New Orleans. I am not for a minute putting down the other well known cities of jazz, but it just had a particular sound in New Orleans. Pete Fountain and Al Hirt used to guest star often on Johnny Carson's *Tonight Show*. I noticed that Doc Severinson, a fine musician in his own right, always waited for them to set the beat. That tells me that New Orleans jazz has a unique and seemingly indefinable sound, along with its own special beat. This book is about how that special beat has always survived in New Orleans.

THE ORIGINS OF JAZZ

Eubie Blake and "Jelly Roll" Morton had several things in common. Each got their start playing the piano in sporting houses, Eubie in Baltimore and "Jelly Roll" Morton at Storyville in New Orleans, but both were around for the beginning of jazz. We all tend to believe jazz started in New Orleans, but that is not totally true. In America it did start there, but it began long before in far away places. Just as it was for people, New Orleans was a melting pot for jazz. Eubie began his career in the pre-jazz era of ragtime. Scott Joplin was famous for writing ragtime music and Eubie could really play Joplin's music. He also composed some of his own.

The fundamental earthy rhythms of early jazz had come from Africa with the slaves. When they danced to their own music in Congo Square, the sound was contagious, and in some strange fashion, it always had a certain association with voodoo. Some of the dance rituals of voodoo were incorporated into jazz also. A little of that influence still lingers today. Probably at least half of the jazz musicians still keep a few talismans or voodoo charms around.

"Jelly Roll" Morton tried to say he invented jazz, which was not quite true, but he was influential early on. He recreated the rhythms of ragtime and was an innovator, in that he blended ragtime and rhythms and added new instruments which also blended into jazz. Morton and his band, the Red Hot Peppers, made early jazz recordings in Chicago. Before returning to New Orleans, Morton performed in Washington D.C., New York, and Harlem.

The introduction of brass instruments added a new dimension to jazz and became the source of several local stories. One story revolves around a Mexican band that performed in New Orleans. Allegedly, local musicians were so enamored by the brass instruments that they offered to buy them. The Mexicans were only too happy to comply because they could sell the instruments at a good price, return to Mexico, and replace them cheaply. More about this later on.

"Jelly Roll" Morton & His Red Hot Peppers, 1926, Chicago. L-R: Omer Simeon, Andrew Hiliare, John Lindsay, Johnny St. Cyr, "Kid" Ory, and George Mitchell; Seated: "Jelly Roll" Morton • Hogan Jazz Archive, Howard-Tilton Memorial Library, Tulane University

Original Dixieland Jazz Band, ca. 1917. L-R: Tony Sbarbaro, Eddie Edwards, Nick LaRocca, Larry Shields, and Henry Ragas. • Hogan Jazz Archive, Howard-Tilton Memorial Library, Tulane University

It is well known, however, that a lot of military band instruments could be bought cheaply after the Civil War. The minstrel shows became so popular that they too played a part in the development of jazz. Their banjo music was adopted by jazz bands, just as the army bugle was replaced by the cornet. Both instruments lent themselves to the boisterous sound of jazz.

And how, you might ask, did jazz get its name? Apparently F. Scott Fitzgerald used "Jazz" in reference to the 1920s. In his mind, "Jazz" described the fast moving life en vogue during that historic era, therefore, he called it The Jazz Age. Fitzgerald did not know jazz was a word used in Congo Square that had a sexual connotation. Well, all in all it was pretty sexy music. Ragtime became extremely fashionable. I tried to imitate my cousin dancing the Charleston. My mother and aunt wore knee-length Georgette dresses with broad sashes tied around their hips. Huge hats sat on top of fancy hair styles built on "rats" (rolls of fibrous stuffing). The result was a circle of hair puffed out under the edge of wide hats. It was the "Gibson Girl" style. Nevertheless, the name Jazz stuck but some bands spelled it Jass. The Original Dixieland Jazz Band was white; however, they modeled the Dixieland sound after New Orleans black jazz bands and took it to New York, where it was first recorded. The predominant sound came from brothels in Storyville, the red-light district where jazzmen created it.

STORYVILLE

It must be recognized that Storyville played a rollicking part in the fortunes of New Orleans jazz musicians. By 1885, brothels began to appear in considerable numbers, especially in the French Quarter and Basin Street area. About 1890, the voice of opposition to rampant and uncontrolled vice began to make itself heard. However, little was done until 1897 when Alderman Sidney Story, familiar with methods used in European cities to control prostitution, introduced an ordinance to confine the spread of prostitution. The city council adopted the ordinance. It is a matter of history that the area was thus referred to as Storyville.

The brothels provided musical entertainment for their customers and the best homes possessed ballrooms and regularly employed orchestras. This created employment for all jazz musicians. Lulu White, who resided at 235 North Basin Street, was one of the more famous Madams. White enlisted octoroon women and appropriately referred to her place as Mahogany Hall. She was apparently favored in her tax assessment for she only paid $300 a year, whereas competitor Madge Leigh, situated on Custom House Street, paid $1,200. Sumptuously furnished, brothels often contained Persian rugs, antique furniture, porcelain lamps and finely decorated jardinieres complete with ferns and palms.

Jitney dances were a popular way for the house to make money. A man would buy a ticket for a dime. When he danced with a girl, she would be given a ticket. At the end of the evening, tickets were turned in and the girls were paid a percentage. If a man wanted to dance with the same partner all evening, he had to buy a whole long string of tickets and could dance as long as the tickets held out.

From the Collection of The Louisiana State Museum

Wilma Burt's "Mirror Ballroom," 1902-1903. • From the Collection of The Louisiana State Museum

Another style of band originated about the time Storyville was in its robust days. Referring to themselves as "spasm bands," these itinerant bands played on street corners, in saloons, and the cheaper brothels. It was the spasm band that introduced the kazoo.

In his book *The French Quarter*, Herbert Asbury describes the first spasm band. The original organizer was Harry Gregson, who was also the outfit's singer. Gregson couldn't afford a megaphone so he crooned through a piece of gas pipe. Emile Lacomb, called Stalebread Charley, played a fiddle made from a cigar box. Willie Bussey, know as Cajun, played the harmonica. Charley Sein invented the use of an old kettle, a cowbell, and a gourd filled with pebbles as kinds of traps. Eventually Sein became a well-know drummer. Chinee slapped a bull fiddle made from half a barrel and later exchanged it for a coffin-shaped contraption built by the boys. Three other band members, Warm Gravy, Whiskey (Emile Benrod), and Monk (Frank Bussey), played whistles and various horns and apparently the kazoo, which were made at home. They called themselves The Razzy, Dazzy Spasm Band and were said to be the first to yell "Hi-de-hi," and "Ho-de-ho." When Sarah Bernhardt visited New Orleans, Gregson and his band serenaded the French actress.

VOODOO
MARIE LAVEAU

(born ca. 1794, New Orleans, Louisiana - died ca. 1881, New Orleans, Louisiana)

Marie Laveau was the Voodoo Queen of New Orleans. After she died, people left little gifts and talismans at her above-ground tomb, a custom that continues today. Marie saved the son of a wealthy New Orleans merchant from going to jail. The young man's father rewarded her with the gift of a house on St. Anne Street between Rampart and Burgundy. To Laveau's followers, her powers seemed to be vested in pure magic. They really believed she had received her powers from God, and as proof placed Christian symbols and icons on the altar during a voodoo ceremony.

Actually, there were two Marie Laveaus, a senior and her daughter, Marie Laveau, Jr. I think it was probably Marie Laveau, Sr. who saved the man's son and got the house. There are also two tombs in the same cemetery.

Laveau had two nephews who played jazz. One was called "Slow Drag" Pavageau. His first name was really Alcide. In later years he played with Sweet Emma Barrett at Preservation Hall. Apparently some of the voodoo had rubbed off on him, for he said spirits walked with him. Pavageau claimed the spirits were not bad and did not worry him. The other nephew, Raymond Glapion, played banjo.

Sometimes white men were curious as to how voodoo worked and would ask to attend the ritual ceremonies which involved snakes, killing chickens, and wild music with the accompanying gyrations, not to mention a lot of red wine, or taffia (sugar cane rum). The onlookers usually ended up bolting for the door to escape the smoke and odors.

However, there were haunting melodies that did come out of these ceremonies and eventually incorporated into the jazz rhythms.

Marie Laveau • Courtesy The Historic New Orleans Collection, Museum/Research Center, Acc. No. 1974.25.23.131

More about Voodoo

Followers sang, danced, and beat drums to a wild song that began with the words "Dance Calinda," carried over from Congo Square. This song is not to be confused with a Cajun country song called "Allons Danser Colinda," which is often played at country dances.

The development of voodooism began with the influx of blacks from Martinique, Guadalupe, and Santo Domingo, but the voodoo priesthood was made up principally of free people of color. The voodoo queens were the priestesses who presided over the ceremonial gatherings and ritual dances. Voodoo doctors also occupied positions in the hierarchy. Both the voodoo priestesses and doctors practiced the art of black magic. The sale of charms, amulets, and magical powders provided a lucrative income.

"Gris-gris" was the magical substance most feared by the superstitious. Gris is the French word for gray, so the feared doom was "double gray." The charm was tied in a little bag of cotton which usually contained powdered brick, yellow ochre, and cayenne pepper. If such a bag was left on one's doorstep, one had to hurry to a voodoo queen and buy a counter-charm, guaranteed to confound the gris-gris.

The voodoo ritual was always totally in the hands of the queen. She could change the routine of the ritual according to her whims, but she had to have the adoration of the serpent as an integral part of the sequence of events. (It was probably a big harmless water snake but the size would have been impressive.)

Several Louisiana authors have described these ceremonies. In one ritual, a drummer sat astride a cypress barrel held together by brass bands, called a tam-tam. He would beat the tam-tam furiously while a male dancer whirled a calabash (a long gourd with the seeds still in it), through the cacophony of the ritual. The entire ritual of pulsating rhythms was calculated to produce a sort of hypnotic trance in the dancing participants, who sang the "Dance Calinda" at a screaming pitch, breaking the silence of the night.

Voodoo rites used to be conducted on Bayou St. John, near the Lake Pontchartrain shore, especially on St. Johns Eve. On sunny mornings, we would take our daughter, Nancy, there to go crabbing. It seemed so peaceful and restful, but the voodoo ceremonies had stopped at that time. Originally the trance inducing rites were held at night amid huge live oak trees heavily hung with Spanish moss, so it was a perfect setting for surreal activities. Rumors were whispered that many wealthy white women used to participate in the erotic dances. Some of the women wore white tignons, but most of the black women preferred tignons made of madras cloth from India, like the bandannas worn by women selling pralines in the Quarter.

And thus, some of the sounds of voodoo rhythms were incorporated into the fabric of jazz. French Lesson: The Creoles used the French pronunciation of "gn" as "ny," thus tignon was pronounced "tin-yon" with the two "n's" so nasalized that you barely heard them.

FIRST IN PRE-JAZZ AND JAZZ

Because they were the first jazz band to record music on celluloid, and the first featured jazz musicians in a movie, The Original Dixieland Jazz Band was undoubtedly the first band to boost jazz music into public vision; however, they were not in Dixieland when it happened. Called the ODJB for short, the band soon became a tremendous success. People in New York heard their music and loved it, but they did not know how to match their feet to the music. They couldn't seem to dance to it and everyone thought it would die a quick death, but in about two days, they figured out what to do with their feet, and no one could stop them. Nick LaRocca, a trumpet player, was the leader of the band. He next took the band to London, and the explosion it caused was something like when the Beatles came here, only in reverse.

Edward "Kid" Ory became a real pioneer in the world of jazz and blues. The "Kid," who played a mean trombone, made the first recording of a black New Orleans band, called Spike's Seven Pods of Pepper Orchestra. Ory apparently developed the light high notes of the trombone, adding a new sound to jazz, and was also a great blues musician. He played in the recording of Louis Armstrong's Hot Five, a band which never existed outside the recording studio.

"Jelly Roll" Morton was the first to smooth and blend the ragtime beat with the sound of jazz. Considered jazz's first great composer, Morton wrote "Mr. Jelly Roll," "The Shreveport Stomp," "The Black Bottom Stomp," and "Milneburg Joys." Milneburg was a sort of resort at the end of the street car line out on Lake Pontchartrain. It was a favorite place for New Orleanians to relax and enjoy life in the summertime. Morton began playing piano in Storyville when he was only ten years old. "Kid" Ory played for him at one time. Morton performed in Washington, D.C., before heading on to New York, but eventually faded away.

W.C. Handy, the King of Minstrelsy, formalized the blues. Handy wrote down music previously passed on by word of mouth. He also composed some outstanding songs, the most famous being "St. Louis Blues." It needs to be said here that Handy never thought of himself as a jazz musician. He, like Eubie Blake, was a product of the pre-jazz "novelty" music. Handy said they played music similar to jazz in the minstrel days, but they did not call it jazz. Minstrel shows began to hire jazz artists and this really helped to make jazz popular.

In 1920, Mamie Smith recorded the first blues song, "Crazy Blues." These early recordings gave blues and jazz great impetus. Sidney Bechet was the first important recorded jazz soloist; Louis Armstrong ran a close second a few months later.

Gertrude Pridgett, known as "Ma" Rainey, was the first important singer to present the classic blues tradition, making blues and early jazz meet.

"Ma" Rainey taught Bessie Smith, who left the minstrel circuit to sing as a soloist. As the first important female jazz singer, Bessie was far ahead of most of her accompanists. It has been said that Fletcher Henderson and Fred Longshaw were the only ones who could do justice to her singing. Smith and Henderson were featured in a movie.

When Duke Ellington opened at New York City's The Cotton Club, jazz was on its way! Ellington made more contributions to jazz than are possible to count. His orchestra was always in the top five, and Ellington ranked with George Gershwin, Cole Porter, and Irving Berlin. He wrote so many songs - thousands - that no one has ever been able to count them. Ellington constantly rearranged his music so that it was always fresh. He first began playing in Washington, D.C., in 1917, learning ragtime. His first composition was "Soda Fountain Rag," and his first concert at Carnegie Hall was in 1943. Jazz was not yet known, but when

W.C. Handy • From the Collection of The Louisiana State Museum

it hit he was ready, opening at The Cotton Club in 1927. Nearly all of the famous jazz artists played with him at one time or another. Duke Ellington was truly a national treasure.

The Assunto brothers, Frank and Fred, were just kids when all of this was going on. By the time the brothers were teenagers, they wanted a band of their own to play Dixieland music. The brothers talked their father, "Papa Jack," into playing with them. "Papa Jack" later became their manager. Calling themselves the Dukes of Dixieland, the band opened in 1948. For 44 consecutive months, they played at the Famous Door. The Assuntos had a lot to do with preserving the trombone; "Papa Jack" played trombone and banjo. Gradually other musicians joined the band. The Dukes of Dixieland could play slow, lowdown gut struts or fast jive with a swing that left dancers exhausted. It was said the Assuntos could almost blow a man head over heels backwards, they blew such a hot horn.

Tragically, Fred died a premature death in 1966, followed by Frank in 1974. Some of the members tried to reconstitute the band but it was never the same. "Papa Jack" retired to teach music, and died in 1985. Nevertheless, they remain a bright spot in everyone's memories of Dixieland jazz.

INSTRUMENTS

BUGLE (VALVELESS)
TRUMPET
CORNET
FLUGELHORN
POCKET TRUMPET
TROMBONE
SOPRANO CLARINET
BASS CLARINET
SAXOPHONE
TENOR
ALTO
BARITONE
SOPRANO
WOODWINDS: BASSOON, OBOE, NAGASWAREN, FLUTE
DRUMS: CYMBALS, TOM-TOMS, SNARE DRUM, BASS DRUM (USED WITH DRUMSTICKS, MALLET, BRUSHES, ETC.)
VIBRAPHONE (METAL BARS)
MARIMBA (WOODEN BARS)
CONCERT GRAND PIANO, HAMMOND ORGAN, VARIOUS KEYBOARDS
STRINGS: VIOLIN, CELLO, BASS, KORA (WEST AFRICAN) ELECTRIC BASS, GUITAR, TWIN NECKED GUITAR (GIBSON)

12

WHAT THESE INSTRUMENTS DO FOR JAZZ

In the traditional jazz band the trumpet or the cornet carries the melody, much as a soprano singer does, and the heavier, richer sound of the trombone punctuates the melody from underneath the sound of the cornet. The rhythm is kept steady by the percussion instruments, the drums, tom-toms, cymbals, gourds and any sort of trap.

The deep throated hum of the bass fiddle holds the sound together and the guitar, banjo, or piano, having the ability to create chords, provide a fundamental structure which can round out the total sound of the piece of music.

Since the early days, jazz has always offered musicians great freedom, before any other type of music did, to improvise and create as they played, and they were in love with this new free music which gave them a chance for personal expression. Anyone who was introduced to jazz and could play it, instantly became ecstatic over the infinite possibilities. Louis Armstrong lifted improvisation to new and unimaginable heights, and every musician who plays jazz today is beholden to him for that gift.

MORE ABOUT THE MUSICAL BEGINNINGS

It would be hard to name all the countries whose natives brought their rhythms to America, but we will examine some of them. The Cuban population included many African and Spanish people who blended their musical rhythms. Trinidad had the steel drum bands which produced the most energetic rhythms. Calypso music combined the sounds of West Africa, Spain, and France. Haiti is probably most responsible for the voodoo music, as well as the superstitions that so many jazz musicians hung on to.

The blues was an entirely different style of music and came from the sounds of workers singing in the fields and calling to each other, sometimes called "field hollers." That was combined, strangely enough, with Christian hymns and harmonies. Almost everyone who practiced voodoo also embraced Christianity, and there were always Christian icons and symbols on the voodoo altars. Blues music has always seemed to soothe people going through hard times. It has a deep meaning for them that most of us will probably never completely understand, but it is powerful music. The field workers sang as they worked and probably did a lot of improvising. They always hung on to their God for solace, and they always hung on to their music. When jazz came along, it provided a cheerful happy sound that made one want to dance, so it was natural that blues and jazz sometimes got mixed up.

Another brand of music arrived from Brazil where a blend of African music, European folk songs, Brazilian dance rhythms of the Samba, and music of street festivals were combined. It was an exciting music with a throbbing beat, and it certainly contributed to jazz music.

The number of nationalities to be found in this new world in the 18th century is almost unbelievable. Included were French, Spanish, English, Scottish, Irish, Italians, Germans, Slavics, Asians, and Africans from many different tribes.

The dances of these various peoples included jigs, hornpipes, flamencos, square dances, and African slave dances. There were also many different songs such as sea chanteys and work songs from both black and white sailors, from roustabouts, and even from Gaelic tunes. There had been brass bands in European villages. Some of the West African ritual dances were interspersed with high pitched yells and whoops, which could carry over long distances. We find a similar effect in yodeling, which was invented to carry sound a long way over the Alps.

It may seem odd to mention Asian music in a book about jazz. It did not affect jazz much, but its spiritual principles were sometimes attractive to the performers. We forget that much of West Africa was under Asian control, and some of the music carried over. They seemed to have similarities to some of the voodoo spiritual beliefs. In recent times many musicians, including the Beatles, have made pilgrimages to gurus in Asia. It seems that all music has a connection to the very soul of the performer.

MARCHING BANDS

After Bob and I married, we lived with his mother in a large house on the corner of Carrollton Avenue and Hickory Street in New Orleans. There was a chain link fence around the backyard, and when our daughter Nancy was about two years old, she spent a lot of time playing out back and talking to people who passed the gate.

A church stood on Hickory Street several blocks from Carrollton in the direction of the Mississippi River. Several more blocks away was a cemetery. When a funeral was held at the church, it was an all day celebration of the individual's life. In addition to hymns and prayers, many testimonials were given. They told everything about the person's life - good and bad. After the preacher talked, a final viewing was held and everyone passed by the coffin. Then they hoisted the coffin into the hearse and a parade march led the procession to the cemetery. A band wearing derbies or top hats came next, followed by the hearse. Usually, the Sisters of the church dressed in white, came next. As the procession marched down Hickory Street toward the cemetery, they passed our yard. Nancy would hang on that fence and watch them from the time they came in view until they were totally out of sight. The Grand Marshal led the parade and wore a broad satin sash over his shoulder and across his chest, held by a large rosette on the opposite hip. The name of the band or the church society was emblazoned on the sash and usually had a border of purple satin or gold braid. The Grand Marshal strutted with a long baton while the band played a mournful hymn in the cadence of a slow dirge. On the way to the cemetery, everyone walked very slowly and solemnly. Often they played "Just a Closer Walk with Thee."

After they "turned loose the body" (a local expression) and put the casket down, they marched back to the church, which was a whole different scene. They were jazzing up their steps and whirling around and the band was playing ragtime and jazz. Everybody had a good time. They particularly liked to play "Oh, Didn't He Ramble" and "When the Saints Go Marching In." Sometimes, the band even played a song called "I'm Glad You're Dead, You Rascal You!" I thought it was wonderful, a real celebration of life for the person who died, as well as their own lives. Music is just good medicine for people.

George Williams Band • Courtesy The Historic New Orleans Collection, Museum/Research Center, Acc. No. 96-36-L

MARCHING BANDS
...continued

When a jazz musician died in New Orleans, the funeral march was huge. They often laid his musical instrument on top of the casket. There were also marching bands that just liked to parade for any occasion. In either case, there was a "second line" of marchers dressed in fancy clothes, hats, and decorated parasols following behind the band, strung out in a long line.

After we moved to the country, we found there were many benevolent societies in the black community, which paid for visits to the doctor and saw to it that every member was properly buried. These organizations had wonderful names like "The Sunflower Society," and "The Good Brothers," but the best was "The Young Men's and Ladies' Society" of which most of the members were seventy or eighty years old, so you know how long they had been in existence.

An annual celebration was held on the society's anniversary date. They would hire a marching band. The society in Hillaryville was the best, although not as fancy as the New Orleans societies. This small settlement was founded many years ago by free people of color. Everyone wore white clothing. The brothers wore white suits, the sisters wore white uniforms with either white hats or white tignons on their heads. Tignons are large kerchiefs, usually tied in the front with the points sticking out sideways. The little girls wore white dresses with red hats, and the little boys wore white shirts and pants and red baseball caps. It was a lovely sight to see them come marching down the River Road and the music was great. Lots of cars of young people would often respectfully follow behind the parade, just to hear the music, and some of us would walk up on the levee and watch them go by.

When the bands march in the city of New Orleans, they grow even more spectacular. They often march for social and fraternal organizations that are just out for the fun of it. All of the clothing is color coordinated and the band uniforms are spectacular. The members spend really big money to belong to these groups and to buy the fancy suits and dresses. These bands are always "brass" bands, emphasized in the name. The Grand Marshal gets out a brass whistle to sound the signal. The second line snaps to and immediately falls in behind the band. Those in the second line wear ornaments of great color – ribbons and sashes, and colorful umbrellas decorated with flowers and glitter, with frills around the edge and ribbons streaming from the points. If you have never seen this, you haven't lived life to the fullest.

Eureka Brass Band • Courtesy The Historic New Orleans Collection, Museum/Research Center, Acc. No. 96-36-L

A List Of Some Marching Bands

Olympic Brass Band
Eureka Brass Band
Young Tuxedos Brass Band
Majestic Brass Band
Pin Stripe Brass Band
All Star Brass Band
Rebirth Brass Band
Algiers Brass Band
Chosen Few Brass Band
Reward Brass Band
Onward Brass Band
Reliance Brass Band
Holy Ghost Brass Band
Imperial Brass Band

EUBIE BLAKE

(b.1883, Baltimore, Maryland - d.1983, New York, New York)

There was only one Eubie! You didn't have to say his last name. I have always admired him and enjoyed watching him on television. I use to wonder if I would ever get to see him when he came to New Orleans.

After we bought Tezcuco Plantation on the Old River Road near the Sunshine Bridge, many people came to visit. The last ten years we lived there, we opened the house for tours. Our home was filled with old New Orleans style furniture, and people enjoyed it. Bob had semi-retired and was working up at the Greenwell Springs Tuberculosis Hospital.

One evening I was sitting on the side of our big tester bed with my feet on the bed steps, watching the *Tonight Show* when Eubie Blake was a guest. I had seen him on the program before and he was always very funny. Johnny Carson was teasing him a little that night. Eubie lived in Brooklyn in New York with his wife Marian. Johnny asked him why he had never moved out of that neighborhood, since he had made a lot of money. Eubie said, "Well Marian owned the house and I just decided to coop with the chicken." I sat there with my feet on the bed steps, thinking how much I would like to meet him. The following story, I swear is not made up. The next morning at about 8:00 a.m. I got a call from Vaughn Glasgow, a very good friend who is curator of special exhibits at the State Museum in New Orleans, and is a profound jazz buff. He said he wanted to bring some friends up to see our plantation house. I said, "Surely Vaughn, you know you don't have to ask me. Just come." He said, "Well, this will be a very special visit. Eubie Blake is coming to New Orleans and his wife, Marian, would like to see some plantation houses." Eubie was going to perform on the boat *The President* while in New Orleans. I couldn't believe my wish had been answered so quickly!

Al Rose & Eubie Blake, 1977 • Hogan Jazz Archive, Howard-Tilton Memorial Library, Tulane University

More about Eubie

On the morning they were due to come, I got to thinking about Lester Delmore, who had worked for us for thirty years. He played guitar and harmonica, but his father had played those instruments plus the banjo and fiddle. I said, "Lester, why don't you come to lunch with us. I think Eubie would like to talk to you." He said that kind of company was too fancy for him, and I said it wasn't going to be fancy at all, just plain folks, so he went home, changed out of his work clothes, put on a white shirt, and he was ready.

Eubie arrived and Marian was a darling person, just charming, and smart. She was Eubie's agent. They told me she was a really astute business woman. She was in her eighties, but Eubie was in his nineties. We toured the house and they were told that the plan was to take them to The Cabin restaurant and then tour Houmas House. We called Lester, and Eubie immediately adopted him. Vaughn and Mary Tunis were with them, along with Al and Diana Rose, who were steeped in jazz. Eubie went all the way back to the ragtime age and knew so much about all phases of jazz. He was still active and alert and could remember a million stories. He loved to joke around, but he was obviously not too steady on his legs, and was quite fragile. He grabbed Lester's arm and hung on in order to steady himself. He never let go of Lester the rest of the day. Al Rose remembered how Eubie petted the sides of the cabin and said that was the kind of house he grew up in. He said he felt at home there. At lunch he sat next to Lester and they immediately had their own conversation going.

Of course, Eubie used to come to St. Louis and Memphis a lot to play music, and then he would go down to New Orleans. Lester explained that all those musicians used to play on riverboats coming down to New Orleans. His father knew some of them and had bought all of their records so Lester was familiar with the name of everyone Eubie was talking about. Eubie and Lester sat there and traded stories for the rest of the meal. He would lean over to tell Lester stories that he didn't want Marian to hear, about a few of his early flings with girls, and then they would laugh so hard. Marian was said to be very jealous, even of Eubie's first wife who had died. He was said to have been quite a ladies' man in his younger days. Al Rose, in his book *I Remember Jazz,* tells of asking Eubie when he was 97 years old, "How old do you have to be before the sex drive goes?" Eubie replied, "You'll have to ask somebody older than me."

I have wished a thousand times I had taken a tape recorder to capture the stories about the jazz musicians. Of course, Eubie had started in the pre-jazz age playing and composing ragtime pieces, but he could really play jazz. He was not from New Orleans, but loved the music there and used to visit there often in his earlier years.

The night he did his show on the boat we all went down to hear him. Vaughn led him up to the stage and he looked so small and frail, going up the steps, but the minute he sat down at the piano he shed a good twenty years and looked like he could live forever. I watched his fingers flying over the keys and when he came back and sat down I said, "You must not have any arthritis." He said, "Oh yes I do. Didn't you see me flexing my fingers in between numbers to keep them limber?" He lived to be just barely a hundred years old.

Al eventually put together a book of all his stories, called *Eubie.* As I listened to him several times on the Carson show, I was amazed at how cool he was. He had lived through a lot of different phases of black and white relationships, and he had always stayed so dignified and rocked with the boat, seemingly knowing that someday everything would change.

Eubie was known as the last living link to ragtime. He remembered the cakewalk but didn't dance it. He said his dancing was "buck dancing," where you sprinkled a little sand on the floor and sort of shuffled the feet. It sounded like "soft shoe" dancing to me. He wrote "The Charleston Rag" in 1899 and became famous for all of the songs he wrote for Broadway shows in the 1920s. He made a big comeback in the 1960s and recorded a double LP, *The Eighty-Six Years of Eubie Blake*. That created a demand for him to appear everywhere. Suddenly everyone wanted to hear the old ragtime music.

His parents had been slaves and were manumitted at the end of the Civil War. His father took the name of Blake from his former master. After the war, Eubie's father continued to work for Blake. His name was just John and he took the middle name of Sumner because he liked the sound of it. Eubie had music in his heart and soul from the time he was a little boy and his parents scraped to buy him a little pump organ.

His mother was a God-fearing woman, liked church hymns and no devil's music. She told him to "Take that ragtime out of my house." That was the first time Eubie knew he was playing ragtime. He played in a small band, but they were playing "white music," which bored him. When he played his favorite chords the leader told him, "You don't play that ragtime in my band," so he left the band. Eubie had learned something else; ragtime was his kind of music.

Eubie Blake, 1979 • Hogan Jazz Archive, Howard-Tilton Memorial Library, Tulane University

More about Eubie

On his own, Eubie found a job, but he was just a kid. At night after his parents had gone to bed, Eubie would slip out to play piano at a bawdy (brothel) house. To play there, Eubie had to look older than he was, so a pair of long pants were kept on hand for him to change into. Brought up to be a gentleman, Eubie never liked to cuss or use words like whorehouse or brothel, so he coined the name "hook shops." When his parents caught him sneaking out, they discovered the young musician had made more money than they had ever seen. Recognizing Eubie's love for music and a need to work, his father allowed him to keep the job.

In 1921, Eubie and Noble Sissle met. Finding they worked together well, the duo put on a show called *Shuffle Along*. It was the first African-American musical to be put on Broadway, and it was a colossal success. They grossed almost $8 million, which was unheard of at that time. Eubie celebrated by buying himself a full-length raccoon coat he was pretty proud of.

Eubie was married to his first wife, Avis Lee, for 28 years when she died. In 1945 he married Marian Gant Tyler, a good looking musical show girl who came from a good family. Her husband had been a well known musician, and she had worked as a secretary to W.C. Handy, the Minstrel King. After Eubie and Marian married, she became his agent, supervising his work, time, and interviews. In addition to scheduling appointments and negotiating contracts, Marian bought Eubie's clothes, oversaw the banking, and answered the phone (he never did). Once Mary Tunis asked Marian what kind of conversations she and Eubie had (because she hadn't heard any) and Marian said, "Eubie doesn't take any part in conversations, he just declaims," and Mary realized she was absolutely right.

I have given a lot of space in writing about Eubie, even though he wasn't a New Orleans musician, but he did so love New Orleans and came there so often that he thought about moving there in his later years, but it never happened. He was so important in the early years of jazz and was not only talented, but was helpful to others. He never lost his sense of humor, which is probably why he lived so long. His mother had lost nine babies in birth before Eubie came along. They thought they would never have a child, but when they got Eubie, they really got a keeper. (Read Al Rose's book, *Eubie*.)

AL & DIANA ROSE

I had heard of Al Rose, but had never met him until he came up with Eubie. I was aware of his books about jazz and Storyville. I later discovered that his wife, Diana, who was a classically trained musician, knew as much about jazz as he did and could play anything on the piano. Vaughn Glasgow called on a pretty summer day and asked if he and Diana could come and picnic on the grounds at Tezcuco. I was always glad to see Vaughn. They brought friends from England whom they intended to introduce to New Orleans jazz. Al could not come that day, but I later learned that he probably knew just about every jazz musician in the United States and had booked them into clubs and concert halls, arranged recording sessions, taken care of them when they were sick, and hired them to do such things as painting or plastering when they were down and out and couldn't get a gig. Al occasionally sat in with them and played a little.

Al Rose, 1982, (detail) • Hogan Jazz Archive, Howard-Tilton Memorial Library, Tulane University

Diana and her friends had put a fine gourmet picnic together, and we had a lovely visit. Her teenage son was along and was as personable as his parents. After the picnic, Diana's son picked up everything and took it out to the car, way in the front parking lot. We had a pet deer at the time. The neighbors had brought us an abandoned fawn, and she was in a pen near the back of the house. Diana's son came back, marching up the sidewalk and blowing his bagpipes. Vaughn said, "Look at the deer." She was listening to the strange bagpipe music as if she couldn't believe what was happening and her ears were pricked up so high she almost looked like a mule deer. She didn't know how she added to the entertainment that day. It was a lovely afternoon even though Al had not been able to come along.

At Christmas time Mary Tunis, whom I met when Eubie came up, called and invited me to a party at her apartment and to spend the night. This was after Bob died and I was about ready to test my new life of having to go it alone, so I readily accepted. When I arrived, she told me Al and Diana Rose were coming. She said, "Al doesn't like to go to parties. He will come just to be nice to me, but I know he won't stay long." He came and I had a good visit with him, for he was always a very gregarious and entertaining conversationalist. The Roses, Vaughn, and I sort of stayed in our little circle, having a fine time. Suddenly Al said, "Well, I'm going to leave. Come on over to our house and we'll visit some more." I said, "Oh, I can't. I'm Mary's house guest and I'm spending the night with her." He said, "Oh, she won't care and we'll take Vaughn with us and he can bring you back." So he dragged me in the other room, still protesting, and told Mary we were leaving. She said that was fine, so we all took off.

It was a great experience, sitting in comfortable chairs in a large but cozy room, and listening to snatches of music. Al had stacks of sheet music, some quite old, and Diana played anything we wanted to hear. The conversation turned to early Creole African music, voodoo, and the old Congo Square of slavery times. Someone mentioned the Bamboula, a song named for the Bamboula tambourine. They always played it when they had their dances in Congo Square. Diana said, "Would you like to hear it?" I didn't even know anyone knew that music anymore, but Louis Moreau Gottschalk had written a song which I presume was taken from the original sound. I had always imagined it must have been loud, stomping music with a heavy beat, but when Diana played it without all the drum beating, it was the loveliest, sweetest music I had ever heard.

The evening had been so great, but we soon realized it was 2:00 in the morning and I said, "We need to go back. Mary will have to let me in." Al said, "No, call her and tell her to come here." So I called and Mary was still up and around, cleaning up after the party, but she said, "I have had a little too much wine tonight, I don't think I should drive." Al said, "Vaughn, go get her," and Vaughn did, so we continued with more talk of jazz and ragtime and old music. Apparently, Al never took "no" for an answer. That evening was one of the great memories of my life.

Al had manufactured his own definition of jazz as "any known melody collectively improvised upon by two or more musical voices in 2/4 or 4/4 time, and syncopated." I asked Diana to repeat his definition to me over the phone and I wrote it down in my telephone/address book, because I never wanted to forget it. Al is no longer with us, but he won't soon be forgotten.

L-R: Al Rose, Blue Lu Barker, Harry Shields, Chink Martin, Sherwood Mangiapane, and Joe Mares, Jr. • Hogan Jazz Archive, Howard-Tilton Memorial Library, Tulane University

cians stopped, looked it over, and began to talk about it. They understood exactly what I had tried to do. I didn't have to explain a thing. I think it must have something to do with how they see and feel music.

The next morning we arose late, and Mary announced we were going to the jazz brunch at Commander's Palace. It was a crisp, sunny winter morning and nothing could have sounded better. She had reservations in the garden room for us. We sat upstairs looking out into the tops of the giant live oaks in the courtyard. A trio of some really old-time jazzmen were playing and walking around the room. They knew Mary, of course, and the musicians came over to our table. One of the musicians put the mute up to his cornet and leaned over so he was playing softly right in our ears, like a whisper. It was a wonderful morning.

After that Mary announced that we were going to the King Tut exhibit at the New Orleans Museum of Art. I had forgotten to make a reservation early enough and thought I would never get to see it. I asked Mary if we could still get tickets. She told me she was a volunteer and they got tickets for their services so she had them. It was one of the finest weekends I have ever had.

And speaking of art, musicians understand it better than anyone. We had a large tour brought up to Tezcuco one evening and the company bringing them had set up tables in the yard. The tours had pretty well finished when I saw the musicians they had brought along. I asked them if they would like to go through the house while the people were setting up for dinner. They were pleased and they got to a room where a painting of mine was hanging. It was unusual and done in bright colors and it was of our house and gazebo. I had deliberately used colors that would make the objects that should come forward seem to go back, and the spaces that should go back would. These musi-

PRESERVATION HALL

I have already mentioned what a fine thing Allen and Sandra Jaffe and Larry Borenstein did by opening Preservation Hall. You had to get there early if you wanted to sit in a chair because there wasn't room for many people. After the chairs were taken, you either sat on the floor in the front row or stood in the back, but people loved it, so they would stand there for hours. Old-time musicians figured that five was the minimum number of musicians to make up a jazz band. The trumpet (or preferably a cornet) was essential for the big sound, and the group must have a piano and drums. If more musicians could be found, a bass fiddle, guitar, or banjo could be added. Depending upon which musicians were available, the order of priority could be rearranged.

Sweet Emma Barrett was called the "bell gal." She was a regular at Preservation Hall. Actually, the Preservation Hall Jazz Band came to be her band. The band knew all of the old-time music, but they charged extra to play "When the Saints Go Marching In" because so many people asked for it. Emma loved red and usually wore a red "beanie" and often a red skirt or blouse. She always wore a pair of red garters just below the knees or around her ankles. Bells sewn on the garters rang in accompaniment as Emma stomped her feet while playing the piano. In addition to the stomping and bells, she had a blunt, pile driver attack on the piano keyboard. The audience really loved her. As age set in, Emma suffered from arthritis, but continued playing for a long time after that. Near the end of her life, she was playing the piano while sitting in a wheelchair. She just loved to play that jazz.

One night when we were at Preservation Hall, Bob took a picture of the group. On that night the band was a group of men who were famous in the old-time world of jazz and were still playing. Louis Cottrell, Jr. was playing the clarinet, Alcide "Slow Drag" Pavageau was on bass, Jim Robinson was on trombone, and Joe Watkins was on drums. Ernest "Cag" Cagnolotti, also known as Ernie, sat in the front playing trumpet and Emmanuel Sayles was out on the side playing a very large banjo. You will remember from the chapter on Marie Laveau that "Slow Drag" was her nephew. Bob couldn't get Sweet Emma in the same picture because she was way off to the side and he couldn't move around too much in the crowd. I painted a picture later from the photograph Bob took, but didn't finish it until forty years later, when I began to write this book.

Preservation Hall Jazz Band

Louis Cottrell, Sr. played drums for Armand J. Piron's orchestra when they played at the end of Tranchina's Restaurant Pier on the shore of Lake Pontchartrain. The Cottrells and their friends were extremely genteel men, raised in the old Creole tradition. They were very polite to each other and everyone else, plished banjoist and also played a mean guitar. He was a regular at Preservation Hall. He played in a recording session of the Jones-Collins Astoria Hot Eight. It made history because it was the first racially mixed session in the South. Sayless played in a trio for awhile and handed their card to Al Rose.

Jazz fans gather outside the renown Preservation Hall

and spoke with soft voices, different from many of the jazzmen who tended toward the uproarious.

Although Jim Robinson played trombone that night, he originally played guitar. Jim was known to be a very relaxed fellow who didn't worry too much about tomorrow. He was a good trombonist, but had a loose habit of double booking himself, and would then have to get someone to replace him on one of the bookings. In spite of his lackadaisical manner, it was said that once you had established Jim Robinson's presence in a band, you couldn't lose him. His trombone had a pungent, pushing style that was unmistakable. Old-timers said he was a model of traditional "tailgate" jazz. When the band got real happy, he just pitched in and followed along. Robinson told people "If everyone is in a 'frisky' spirit, the spirit gets to me and I can just make my old trombone sing."

Alcide "Slow Drag" Pavageau was a small man with a big bass fiddle, but his playing was renowned. Emmanuel Sayless was an accom-

They called themselves The Three Chocolate Bars. Al questioned the wisdom of identifying the group racially, but Sayless said he was proud to be a Negro and wanted everyone to know it.

Of course there were other bands playing at small places around the Quarter. At night, the music went on into the wee hours. Toney's Spaghetti House stayed open all night because the jazz people, chanteuses and piano players from the night clubs, and the strippers from the "strip joints" didn't knock off until about 2:00 in the morning and then they were starving. He did a good business with show people, and local folks and tourists who stayed out late could always find a place to eat.

Big bands from Chicago and New York played at places like the Blue Room at the Roosevelt Hotel (now the Fairmont). The bands finished by midnight and went down to the small clubs in the Quarter, where they jammed with the local jazzmen, and everyone proceeded to "pass a good time," as the Cajuns say.

EXCURSION STEAMERS

Steamboats and Paddle Wheelers carried party loving people on excursions up and down the Mississippi to Memphis, St. Louis, Kansas City, and across Lake Pontchartrain, carrying jazz right with them, for it was the sound that kept everyone happy.

FOLLOWING IS A LIST OF SOME OF THE EXCURSION BOATS

NATCHEZ
CREOLE QUEEN
CAJUN QUEEN
S.S. ADMIRAL
S.S. DELTA QUEEN
S.S. DIXIE
S.S. GREATER NEW ORLEANS
S.S. MADISON
S.S. MANDEVILLE
S.S. MAJESTIC
S.S. MISSISSIPPI
S.S. NEW CAMELIA
S.S. PRESIDENT
S.S. ROBERT E. LEE
S.S. ST. PAUL
S.S. SIDNEY
S.S. SUSQUEHANNA

DIZZY GILLESPIE

(b.1917, Chewraw, South Carolina - d.1993, Englewood, New Jersey)

My husband and I went down to a medical convention at the old Jung Hotel on Canal Street, at about the time the ancient rules on enforced segregation were beginning to break up, but integration was not yet fully accepted. Before the convention could be held, it was being planned from the headquarters of the organization in Chicago. There would be some doctors of African lineage and they were trying to find a hotel that could work things out for a "mixed group." The planners flew down from Chicago to arrange the details and the Jung Hotel offered a dining room on the top floor where the banquet would be very private and everything would be hunky dory. We sat with a doctor and his wife from New Orleans, and had more in common to talk about with them than we would have had with many of the doctors from the North.

Al Hirt's club had been rented for the evening's entertainment so the doors would be closed to all outsiders. Hirt was out of town and our entertainer for the night was Dizzy Gillespie. Dizzy was not from New Orleans, but he came down to the city a lot and was loved there. As he started to play, I noticed Bob was staring at him as if he were diagnosing a patient. Finally he said, "Look at Dizzy's neck. He has dissected the neck muscles away from the outer skin because he blows so hard and has forced the air that far back." Sure enough, when he played you could see that the air was not only in his cheeks, but it was bulging out all the way around to the back of his neck, from the air forced in between the muscles and skin of his neck.

Dizzy's father had encouraged his enthusiasm for music.

He won a scholarship to Carolina's Laurinburg Institute and had some formal training in both trumpet and piano. Someone fell on Dizzy's trumpet once and bent the bell part of it upward. He said the sound came to him sooner that way and he liked it, so he had a trumpet purposely designed in that style. It was his trademark and now other musicians use it. It is really quite a distinguished looking piece of equipment and is called an oblique trumpet. Jazz devotees believe Dizzy was the greatest jazz trumpeter that ever lived. Very few other trumpeters have been able to recreate his style. However, it would not be fair to compare his technique to that of Louis Armstrong, for Dizzy was of a later age and a newer style of jazz. He helped invent be-bop music, and introduced Afro-Cuban music into jazz. It has been said that harmonically he was ahead of everyone in his age bracket. Thankfully, he made a huge number of recordings.

Dizzy Gillespie • From the Collection of The Louisiana State Museum

AL HIRT and PETE FOUNTAIN

Al Hirt (b.1922, New Orleans, Louisiana - d. 1999) Pete Fountain (b.1930, New Orleans, Louisiana)

Al Hirt and Pete Fountain both grew up in the New Orleans area and were both fine musicians, but they were just coming into their own when jazz was falling on hard times. Al played a hot trumpet and Pete played a cool clarinet. There were not many places to work and the younger musicians were getting all the jobs because young people wanted a new sound. Al and Pete got so desperate they took jobs as bug exterminators. They looked around the country and found new audiences in places where the old timers still appreciated true jazz. They were making the rounds in Las Vegas and appearing on Johnny Carson's *Tonight Show*. For awhile Pete played a regular spot on the *Lawrence Welk Show*, and that contributed to his fame. Hirt had studied classical trumpet at the Cincinnati Conservatory and was sometimes believed to be overqualified for Dixieland music, but his audiences didn't think so. Fountain played with the Junior Dixieland Band in New Orleans, was much influenced by Benny Goodman, and later learned a lot from being in Phil Zito's Basin Street Six. Al and Pete played together quite often and eventually both opened their own night clubs in New Orleans' French Quarter. Pete played nightly at a new night club called the Rainforest. It was on top of the new Hilton Hotel, situated on Poydras at the river. They had sound and light effects of thunder and lightning to add to the excitement of the rainforest, which was hardly necessary with the excitement of Pete's clarinet.

Courtesy Al Hirt

Pete Fountain, ca. 1968 • Hogan Jazz Archive, Howard-Tilton Memorial Library, Tulane University

Pete had a band that always marched in crazy costumes on St. Patrick's Day in New Orleans. He called his band The Half Fast Marching Band. Everyone turned out to see that particular parade but then everyone always loves a parade in New Orleans.

Both of these fine musicians became famous all over the world, and neither one of them ever had to exterminate bugs again.

Pete said he never did think too much about his playing but just played by instinct. He said he blew what he felt and it just seemed to come out right. His comment was, "I don't even read much music, I just read enough not to hurt my jazz." His music was said to be smooth but wild, faithful to the melody line, yet shaped by ad lib solo flights; rompin', stompin', and foot tappin' while gently moody and yet always happy. His band produced what they called "head-arrangements," meaning there were no exact written arrangements for the various instruments. Instead, each side man contributed his own individual interpretation within a general framework of the melody and a rough idea of what the end result should sound like. A favorite saying among jazzmen was "Don't step on my part!"

Al Hirt was a first class jazzman and the word "conformist" was an anathema to all jazzmen. He knew, however, that the learning process and assimilation preceded any individuality. Al studied many of the great jazz artists at an early age. He knew there was no formal school where one could learn jazz. Al became part of the Dixieland restoration. After jazz had been carried all over America and throughout Europe, it began to return more strongly to New Orleans (although it had never completely left) and Al was a big part of that revival.

W.C. HANDY

(b.1873, Memphis - d.1958, New York)

W.C. Handy began to produce blues in a more orderly written form in the early 1900's. His "St. Louis Blues" became famous all over the world. He put on minstrel shows where actors wore makeup that turned the performers into caricatures. They painted huge white circles around their eyes and mouths, grossly exaggerating their features, but making people laugh at how ridiculous they looked. However, they played a lot of wonderful ragtime music and hymns. One of the more famous songs was "Jumpin' Jim Crow." Handy was a bandleader, a composer, and formalized the blues for the first time. They had previously been passed down by word of mouth. He also wrote "Beale Street Blues" and "Careless Love." His shows were very important to the history of jazz because the New Orleans musicians were connected to what he was doing and some of that minstrel music found its way into the rhythms of jazz.

Cakewalks were featured in the minstrel shows and they were dances invented to overstate, thereby making fun of the peculiar way white people were dancing at that time. I remember a phonograph record at my grandmother's house with "The Virginia Cakewalk" on one side. According to Diana Rose, Eubie Blake was the only

W.C. Handy • From the Collection of The Louisiana State Museum

one who remembered what cakewalks looked like, but he couldn't dance, so he couldn't show anyone how to do it.

"Jelly Roll" Morton met Handy in Memphis in the early 1900s and asked the band to play blues for him. Handy said his organization was a minstrel band and could not play that kind of music. "Jelly Roll" said Memphis heard true blues for the first time when Freddie Keppard and his band came up on an excursion boat and played Morton's "New Orleans Blues" for them. When "Jelly Roll" first took his band to New York he made a big hit with "Sergeant Dunn's Bugle Call Blues." The Original Dixieland Jazz Band played Handy's "Beale Street Blues" in the style of a circus band with a slight New Orleans sound. Because of all this coming together of different kinds of music, the blues became very large in Memphis, and the sound lingers there today. As in every other community where blues was played, the field hands and the church choirs took blues into their hearts. The blues still thrive on Beale Street in Memphis.

Eventually W.C. Handy moved from the South to New York, where he opened an office in the Gaiety Theater Building. Handy began to do a lot of bookings for various artists and made a lot of money for them and for himself. He really knew the business end of the music profession. If Handy appeared anywhere, he had to get top billing. It had to say "W.C. Handy, the Father of the Blues."

Al Rose wanted to contact Handy about a business deal once and Eubie told Al Rose he would have to have the money out in his hand and not in his pocket if he wanted to do business with Handy. He said "Put the money out where he can see it." Al went in with what was considered big money in those days and slid it across the desk but Handy said it wasn't enough, so they never sealed the deal.

W.C. Handy Statue on Beale Street in Memphis

Artists portrayed, from left to right are: Jim Robinson (trombone); Joe Watkins (drums); Ernie "Cag" Cagnolotti (cornet); Alcide "Slow Drag" Pavageau (bass fiddle), nephew of Marie Laveau; Louis Cottrell, Jr. (clarinet); Emmanuel Sayles (banjo). Painting by Bobby Potts.

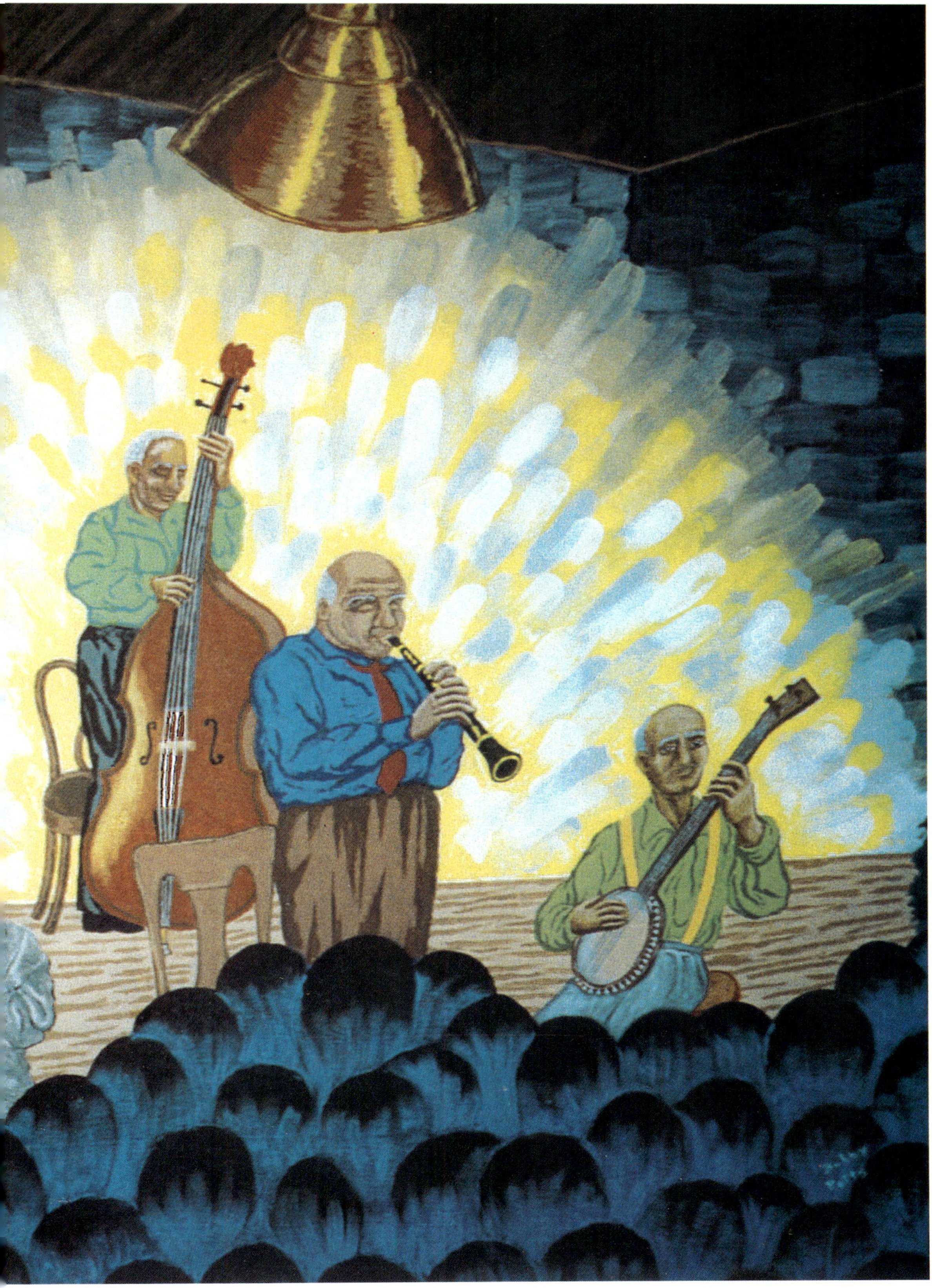

JACK "PAPA" LAINE

(b.1874, New Orleans, Louisiana - d.1966, New Orleans, Louisiana)

"Papa" Laine was really the earliest Dixieland bandleader. His Reliance Brass Band was famous all over New Orleans and the Mississippi Gulf Coast. It was a well respected white band, especially since the early white bands were rare and often did not play as well as the black bands. Older musicians remember that "Papa" sometimes had six of his bands on the streets at one time, during celebrations and festivals. Nick LaRocca worked in some of Laine's bands and when Nick became head of the Original Dixieland Jazz Band, he made sure to put "Paw" Laine in there with him.

The ODJB was a white band that later made a mark of its own in New York. It seems to be a little known fact that two of "Papa" Laine's regular musicians, Achille Baquet and Dave Perkins were very light colored men of part African heritage. It was carried off as a good joke on the audience because nobody could tell what color they were. Laine led the first documentable jazz band in history as early as 1892, and he retired in 1910, before the ODJB became truly famous. Al Rose said he spent many good times with him in the 1950s. Laine lived to be 92 and made a recording for Tulane University when he was 90.

Everyone who writes about him writes in very respectful terms. He was not just a musician; he was a great teacher, and it was the teachers that were so important in the history of jazz.

"Papa" Laine told a story about Mexican musicians coming to New Orleans which should settle the truth about the introduction of brass instruments. Dr. Edmond Souchon, a student of jazz and a jazzman himself, asked "Papa" how he got the instruments for his first band. According to Souchon, Laine said Dave Perkins bought most of the instruments from the Mexican Military Band upon returning home after the 1884-1885 World's Fair, held in the area where Audubon Park is now.

Reliance Band, Standing: Manuel Mello, Alcide Nunez, Leonce Mello, Alfred Laine, Chink Martin, and Mike Stevens. Seated: Jack "Papa" Laine. 1910 • Hogan Jazz Archive, Howard-Tilton Memorial Library, Tulane University

CREOLE PEOPLE

I probably need to do a little explaining here about the term "Creole." A Creole person (of French or Spanish descent) speaks a dialect of French or Spanish. The Spanish term is actually Criolo but everyone uses the term Creole. It can also be taken to mean the same thing for people from any country, including Africa. However, many of the African-Americans were raised with French Creole fathers or worked for Creole families who spoke French, so they truly thought of themselves as Creoles and had a right to.

Creoles were genteel people who had elegant manners and spoke in soft tones because they had been raised to behave in such a manner. Al Rose tells of the first time he met "Jelly Roll" Morton. He said he knew he was looking at a star. He had the bearing and the manner and certainly the clothes. He knew Morton was from New Orleans because he passed by just after lunch time and said "Good Evenin", and only New Orleansians say "Good Evenin" at lunch time.

Marie Laveau would have been called Creole, and many others belonged in this category, including the Lorenzo Tio family, Armand Picou, Peter Bocage, John Casimir, and Paul Barbarin.

LORENZO TIO, JR.

(b.1884, New Orleans, Louisiana - d.1933, New York)

Lorenzo Tio, Jr. was a fine clarinetist and a product of the music that preceded jazz. His family was responsible for teaching Sidney Bechet and so many others. You will not realize how important the Tio family was until you read biographies of all the musicians who studied with them. They taught almost every clarinet player for two generations. The Tios were very honest and if they thought a student was not going to make it, they advised him early on so a lot of money would not be wasted on lessons.

There was Louis "Papa" Tio, a contemporary of Jack Laine, and his famous brother, Lorenzo Tio, Sr., and Lorenzo Jr., who was celebrated in Europe as an "extraordinary clarinet virtuoso." He topped that accolade by introducing the soprano sax to jazz, an extremely demanding instrument that he discovered in France.

The cornet players were always the featured stars of the marching brass bands. Second to them were the really good clarinet players. The stars were members of the Tio family: Alphonse Picou, and George Baquet. Sidney Bechet and several other Tio students went on to become teachers themselves. Armand Piron, whose band played at Tranchina's Restaurant Pier on Lake Pontchartrain, hired Lorenzo, who had by then gained legendary fame. Their theme song was "Dreamy Blues." That song was allegedly published later as "Mood Indigo" under the names of Barney Brigand and Duke Ellington, but people more knowledgeable than I said they knew it was Lorenzo Tio's composition. Tio also played with "Papa" Celestin and Manuel Perez.

Armand Piron was talking to Al Rose one evening and commented on how fellows like Benny Goodman and Tommy Dorsey were getting way ahead of his kind of music. Still, he "allowed as how" when he heard Tio play Liebestraum, he wondered if music ever got any better than that. What a compliment!

ALPHONSE PICOU

(b.ca.1878, New Orleans - d.1961, New Orleans)

Alphonse Picou played clarinet and was one of the famous old-time jazz greats in New Orleans who had played with "Papa" Celestin at the Paddock on Bourbon Street in the Quarter. Walter Blue played trumpet there with him. Sharkey Bonano's band played there at different times too. It has been said that when anyone plays the clarinet solo in "High Society" they are usually imitating the way Alphonse Picou played. Al Rose said Picou always reveled in the flattery of those who imitated his style.

One day some of his friends were trying to get him to play the clarinet, but all he wanted to do was drink. Al said they finally coaxed a young man to play, and that was all it took to get Picou (known as "Pike" to his friends) off the bar stool. He walked over and said, "That ain't the way to do it boy!" and took over the clarinet. He was one of the very early jazzmen, playing the clarinet when he was only twelve years old. He got his start in the business in 1892, when taken in by Boulboul Valentine who led a little known band. Alphonse has been quoted as saying the music played at the turn of the century was not ragtime, simply brass band marching music. He told Al Rose, "It wasn't even ragtime yet, they done some fakin' and taught me how to fake." (Apparently the "fakin" led into ragtime.) He was a part of the Creole Black community and used the French words that everyone begins to use after they have lived in New Orleans for awhile, such as "banquette" for sidewalk and "gallery" for porch.

He got a lot of good experience along the way for he played with "Papa" Celestin's Tuxedo Brass Band and Freddie Keppard's Olympia Band, two of the best ever around. However, I am sure it was a two way street, for he could teach them some things too. He had a face that looked like it should belong to one of the seven dwarfs, for there was always a twinkle in his eyes.

Alphonse Picou, ca. 1945 • Hogan Jazz Archive, Howard-Tilton Memorial Library, Tulane University

FREDDIE KEPPARD

(b.1890, New Orleans - d.1933, Chicago)

Freddie Keppard, the musician who first played the blues for W.C. Handy in Memphis, was considered to be one of the "cornet kings." He came after Buddy Bolton and before "King" Oliver. Keppard and some of his musical relatives grew up in the Tremé Market area on Rampart Street. Eventually, he became the leader of the Olympia Orchestra. He played in an extremely spirited fashion using a sort of staccato phrasing which had been adapted from the style of the New Orleans brass bands. "Jelly Roll" Morton adopted some of those ways. Being a favorite of "Jelly Roll" helped Keppard's reputation tremendously. He went on to play with the original Creole Orchestra when they played on the Orpheum circuit. When they took jazz to Chicago it was said, "that band really upset Chicago and paved the way for the rest of the New Orleans jazzmen." At some point that same band took New Orleans jazz to Los Angeles, so they did a lot to spread the good sound around. Keppard was extremely protective of his style and tried to keep his special secrets from other musicians. As other younger musicians came along and began to surpass him in new styles, he became extremely melancholy and began to drink a lot. He died in Cook County Hospital in Chicago when he was too young to go.

Freddie Keppard, second from right; Lil Armstrong, center • Hogan Jazz Archive, Howard-Tilton Memorial Library, Tulane University

ARMAND J. PIRON

(b.1888, New Orleans, Louisiana - d.1943, New Orleans, Louisiana)

A.J. Piron was unable to walk for years due to a crippling, childhood accident. He focused on studying the violin, playing professionally, and being a popular leader. Piron is most fondly remembered for his band that played at Tranchina's Restaurant at Spanish Fort. He was also a composer and co-formed, for jazz musicians, a publishing company with Clarence Williams. He was leader of Piron's New Orleans Orchestra, which became one of the great orchestras in New Orleans. Some famous musicians played in it, including Lorenezo Tio, Jr. and Louis Cottrell, Sr. Old-timers remember the experience of hearing the melodies of songs like "Purple Rose of Cairo" and "Dreamy Blues" wafting over the waters of Lake Pontchartrain.

Al Rose said Armand was Creole, and told of taking another Creole friend, Peter, to see Armand during his last days. Their greeting, in soft voices was "Evenin' Peter. You looking might prosperous sir. The family fine?" Peter answered "Evenin' Arman.' I hope you res' well this mawnin." It was a typical Creole conversation.

From such an illustration, I hope some of the beautiful relationships that existed in this world of jazz are apparent.

A.J. Piron and His Novelty Orchestra • From the Collection of The Louisiana State Museum
(Piron, far right; Lorenzo Tio, Jr., fourth from right; Louis Cotrelle, drums.)

EDWARD "KID" ORY

(b.1886, Napoleonville, Louisiana - d.1973, Honolulu, Hawaii)

Before forming the first recorded black band, "The Kid" started down the Mississippi River from La Place to New Orleans with the idea of starting his own band, and that was exactly what he did. He first learned to play the banjo, then did a fast run through clarinet, cornet, and alto sax. He finally settled on the slide trombone and formed the Original Creole Jazz Band. He became a successful band leader in New Orleans because he hired the best: "King" Oliver (later replaced by Louis Armstrong) and Sidney Bechet for starters.

"Kid" then moved to California for his health and created Spike's Seven Pods of Pepper Orchestra; the first black jazz band to record. Thus, he carried the jazz movement to the West Coast. His next move was to retire to his brother's chicken ranch in Chicago, but he soon returned. Ory always stayed busy, making records in Chicago, starting another new band in New Orleans at the time of the Dixieland revival in the 1940s, and touring Europe in the 1950s. He finally went farther west, again for his health, and moved all the way to Hawaii. He surprised everyone by coming back to New Orleans for the 1971 Jazz Festival.

"Kid" Ory and George Brunies were said to have perfected the underpinning of a trombone to pull the lighter horns together, which helped the sound of swing as it was coming into vogue. Ory wrote the highly successful music for "Muskrat Ramble." His music was also featured on Orson Welles' radio show. He then worked steadily in Los Angeles writing music for such movies as *New Orleans* and *The Benny Goodman Story*. Some of the band's most requested pieces were "Tiger Rag" (later adopted by Louisiana State University), "Eh La Bas" (Hey Down There), "Mahogany Hall Stomp," "Oh, Didn't He Ramble," and "High Society."

Edward "Kid" Ory • From the Collection of The Louisiana State Museum

OSCAR "PAPA" CELESTIN

(b.1884 Napoleonville, Louisiana - d.1954 New Orleans, Louisiana)

"Papa" Celestin left Napoleonville to play trumpet with the Algiers Brass Band and then with the famous Olympia Brass Band in New Orleans. He later developed his own Tuxedo Brass Band. "Papa" Celestin was one of the most favored leaders of bands in New Orleans and he played at several good nightclubs there.

Then he was not heard from for a good many years, and suddenly he surprised everyone by returning and becoming as popular as ever. His was the band that recorded the famous song "Marie Laveau", and it gave his popularity a big boost. As I have said before, jazz and voodoo were often linked. He became famous all over the country for that song. The young people loved it so well he had a whole new audience. Celestin often played at the Paddock, spelling Sharkey Bonano's band on some nights. That was the small club in the Quarter I mentioned earlier with the "horsey" atmosphere and the horse shoes hung on the wall, free ends up, so one's luck didn't run out. "Papa" had become quite popular again when I was teaching at Tulane University and he was always in demand for college dances.

"Papa" Celestin's Tuxedo Orchestra, 1931. • Hogan Jazz Archive, Howard-Tilton Memorial Library, Tulane University

SIDNEY BECHET

(b.1897, New Orleans, Louisiana - d.1959, Paris, France)

Sidney Bechet was the first important recorded jazz soloist. (Louis Armstrong followed him by making a recording just a few months later.) Sidney did not wish to develop any new styles of jazz, but he always retained his vibrato skills and his enthusiasm for pure jazz. This is not to say he was rigid, for he was a renowned improvisor.

He studied with the great jazz player Lorenzo Tio, Sr., as did many contemporary jazz musicians, and he in turn taught other musicians. He bought a soprano sax on a European visit and found he preferred it to his other instruments. He did a lot of recording in Chicago with diverse artists from New Orleans, Louis Armstrong among them. He went on to play with various orchestras, including Duke Ellington's.

Sidney became a celebrity in Paris and was really better known in France than in the United States. Many of these Creole musicians spoke French and were perfectly at home in Paris. They were also better received in Europe. Bechet also worked with Noble Sissle, the same man who originally teamed up with Eubie Blake to produce the famed show *Shuffle Along*.

Sidney Bechet • Courtesy The Historic New Orleans Collection, Museum/Research Center, Acc. No. 92-48-L, Ford 1562

JOE "KING" OLIVER

(b.1885, New Orleans, Louisiana - d.1938, Savannah, Georgia)

Joe "King" Oliver was a great New Orleans legend. Only part of his talent was put on records. He was originally a trombonist, but he started to play cornet when he was taken into "Kid" Ory's band at Pete Lala's Cafe. When "The Kid" took Oliver into his band, he billed Oliver as "King." Oliver and Ory were in the same age bracket and understood each other only too well.

Many musicians were inspired by Oliver's great talent because he could get so many different sounds out of a trombone. When it came to playing the cornet, his fellow musicians learned about the use of mutes because Oliver was called the master of the various ways to use mutes. He left New Orleans when all the musicians were going up to Chicago to make recordings. For awhile, he joined the band of Bill Johnson at the Dreamland Ballroom. He eventually formed his own band and played at the Lincoln Gardens, and then he brought former student Louis Armstrong (who called him "Papa Joe") up to join the band. Lil Hardin was playing piano and that was where Louis met and married her. "King" Oliver's Creole Jazz Band made some recordings at that time. Oliver said he liked keeping Louis with him playing second trumpet because that way, he was still "The King."

Musicians said the "vocalized" trumpet sound heard in Duke Ellington's Orchestra had been brought in by musicians who had played with Oliver. When Louis Armstrong left Oliver to play with Fletcher Henderson's orchestra, "The King" soon followed him to New York.

"King" Oliver's Creole Jazz Band L-R: Honore Dutrey, Warren "Baby" Dodds, Joe Oliver, Louis Armstrong, Lil Hardin Armstrong, Bill Johnson, and Johnny Dodds • Hogan Jazz Archive, Howard-Tilton Memorial Library, Tulane University

"MA" RAINEY

(b.1886, Columbus, Georgia - d.1939, Georgia)

Gertrude Pridgett was always called "Ma." She was a vocalist and is considered to be the "Mother of the Blues," and she married "Pa" Rainey, so the "Ma" naturally followed. They toured together in the Rabbit Foot Minstrels. She was not a pretty woman, but people said she had a wonderful smile and a lot of gold teeth. Her trademark was that she always wore diamonds, although whether fake or real I wouldn't know.

She became quite well known through her many recordings. She then did some successful shows of her own including *Louisiana Blackbirds*. Her plaintive cry as she wailed the blues sounded something like plain song. (Plain song comes from the early Christian church music and is still used in Roman Catholic and Anglican services. It is sung in free rhythm in the limited Gregorian scale, in unison without accompaniment. Plain song was the source for many hymns.)

"Ma" Rainey was the first important blues singer. A highly successful show called *Ma Rainey's Black Bottom* ran on Broadway years later. It was adapted from a song she used to sing that always stopped the show. "Ma" was a good hearted person who was happy to pass her experience on to others.

"Ma" Rainey & Her Wildcats, L-R: Gabriel Washington, Albert Wynn, Dave Nelson, "Ma" Rainey, Eddie Pollack, and Thomas A. Dorsey • Hogan Jazz Archive, Howard-Tilton Memorial Library, Tulane University

MAMIE SMITH

(b.1883, Cincinnati, Ohio - d.1946)

Mamie Smith's recording of "Crazy Blues" set the jazz world on fire, creating a huge demand for African blues singers and records. She often lost musicians who said she was too "bossy," but she was beautiful and had a fine style of entertainment. She grew very wealthy, wore flashy satin gowns, and came on stage decorated with plumes, feather boas, and feathers on her gowns. She was not very old when she developed a serious arthritic condition. Mamie Smith died in poverty.

BESSIE SMITH

(b.1894, Chattanooga, Tennessee - d.1937, Clarksdale, Mississippi)

Bessie was the greatest blues and jazz singer of all time. They called her "Empress of the Blues," and the title was well deserved. Her powerful, sensual voice impresses people as much today, who hear her records, as her live audiences when she first began. Bessie had such a powerful voice that some said she sounded like a Baptist choir and some said she could produce the sound of a growly deep throated trumpet. She was very dark and strikingly beautiful. Smith became the highest paid black entertainer anywhere.

In 1912, she sang in a show with "Ma" Rainey. "Ma" was impressed enough to take it upon herself to coach Bessie. Although Bessie came along in the same path as "Ma" and Mamie, she surpassed both and paved the way for women blues singers for all time. She often sang with Louis Armstrong and made a big hit with her recording of "Nobody Knows You When You're Down and Out," heralding the Depression Years. She also sang with Fletcher Henderson in New York, and that was about as good a back up as anyone could get. She played at the Apollo Theater and could have made a big comeback, but was killed in a car accident.

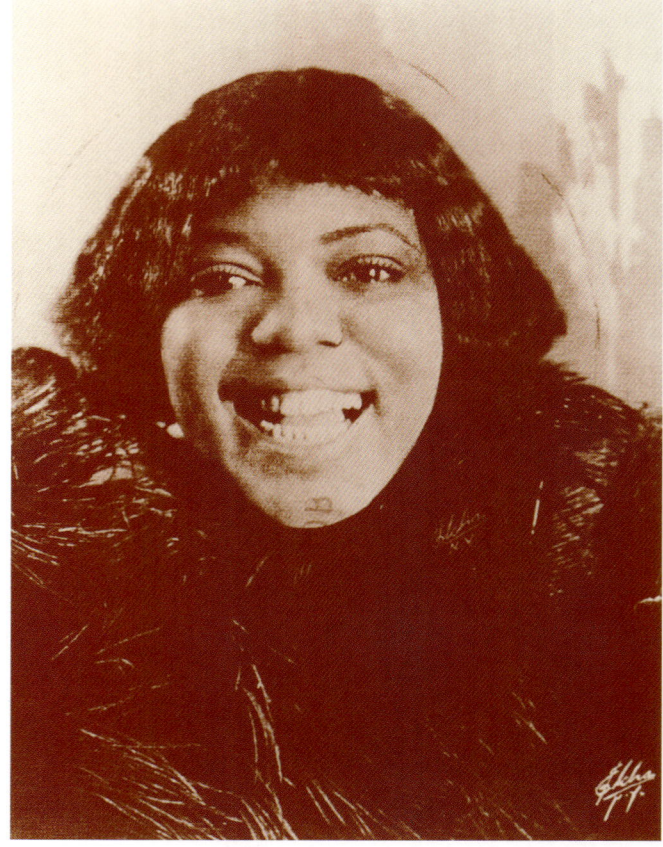

Bessie Smith, ca. 1920s. • Courtesy The Historic New Orleans Collection, Museum/Research Center, Acc. No. 92-48-L, Fold. 3058

LIZZIE MILES

(b.1895, New Orleans, Louisiana - d.1963, New Orleans, Louisiana)

Elizabeth Mary Landreaux Pajaud, otherwise known as Lizzie Miles, was New Orleans' own female jazz vocalist and she became a truly fine classic blues singer. She rose to prominence in the 1920s after she had learned her craft in tent shows and had finally made it into vaudeville. Lizzie was light skinned and beautiful, a true Creole celebrity and more of a cabaret singer. She worked with the best of the jazzmen, men who were already famous: Louis Armstrong, "Kid" Ory, "King" Oliver and "Jelly Roll" Morton. She made recordings with many of them, because she was an asset to any band. As many of the jazz performers did, she toured in Europe. Paris especially loved jazz and they loved her, calling Lizzie the "Black Rose" (La Rose Noire). She too headed for Chicago and New York when all the jazzmen were roaming around the country. After some lean times when blues was slipping, Lizzie again worked with Fats Waller. She sang at the Mardi Gras Lounge on Bourbon Street and at tea dances in the Parisian Room just off Canal Street. They used to host a regular jam session at the Parisian Room every Saturday afternoon, and it was broadcast nationwide on 50,000 watt clear channel station WWL, one of the most powerful stations in the country at that time.

Lizzie made a big comeback singing with Paul Barbarin and Fats Waller in the 1930s. The jazz instrumentalists said they loved her "little Creole songs."

Lizzie Miles, ca. 1953 • Hogan Jazz Archive, Howard-Tilton Memorial Library, Tulane University

HUDDIE "LEADBELLY" LEADBETTER

(b.1885, Mooringsport, Louisiana - d. 1949, Harlem, New York)

"Leadbelly" traveled all over Louisiana and Mississippi with his guitar, trying to make a living as an itinerant singer. He did not know then that he would one day become so important to the history of jazz. The old-timers who really knew about jazz said "Leadbelly" was a "one-man archive." Allegedly, "Leadbelly" kept some 500 songs in his head. Many were passed down from musician to musician. The mental list of music included work songs, prison songs, blues, spirituals, and ballads.

More than once, "Leadbelly" served a stint in prison. Each time he was released, he spent a lot of time in Harlem, playing wherever he could, mostly singing rural songs he had learned from prison. He successfully toured the northern U.S., where he was a sensation, and even performed throughout Europe, but he was most at home when rambling along country roads or city back streets.

His final recording was *Leadbelly's Last Session*, where he played a 12 string guitar. These recordings were made loosely and informally, but they included a voluminous amount of African-American music as it had developed up to and throughout his lifetime. In spite of his hard life, he had a rich emotional sound in his somewhat scratchy voice. He had never changed the sound of the songs to a more modern sound just to play to the current style, so they are about as authentic as anyone could hope for. Although "Leadbelly" was from Louisiana, he never spent much time in New Orleans. He preferred to roam about in lonely places, but the musicians and historians who are students of jazz are beholden to this strange character named "Leadbelly" for what he has contributed to their world. He knew all of the blues and those songs woven into ragtime and jazz, which include "Rock Island Line," "Nobody Knows You When You're Down and Out," "He Never Said a Mumblin' Word," and "Springtime in the Rockies."

"Leadbelly" Leadbetter • From the Collection of The Louisiana State Museum

"JELLY ROLL" MORTON

(b.1885, New Orleans, Louisiana - d.1941, Los Angeles, Califonia)

The thing "Jelly Roll" did best was brag on himself, so many of the things he took credit for had to be taken with the proverbial grain of salt. However, he really was a giant as far as talent went. He claimed he was the one who really invented jazz in 1902. This is not quite true, but in some ways he helped to make it happen by smoothing down the ragtime beat, enhancing some of its components, and liberating the improvisers. "Jelly Roll's" real name was Ferdinand La Menthe, but he took his stepfather's name of Morton because he thought he might be nicknamed "Frenchie." His mother loved opera so he had some background in classical music. "Jelly Roll" also tried trombone, drums, harmonica, guitar, and violin. He apparently was not a very happy person. Other musicians said it was because he was light skinned but not accepted by whites and yet he did not trust blacks. He always carried a gun. It is rather a pity that someone so talented could be so insecure. He did manage to gather some good jazzmen around him and made recordings under the name of the Five Hot Peppers, and under other names.

"Jelly Roll" was a great friend to "Bricktop," a light skinned beautiful black woman with red hair. She went to Paris before she was twenty years old and became a successful cafe owner and hostess. Later on, she opened other night spots including one in Rome. "Bricktop" acquired wealthy friends and members of royalty who loved her. Two of her best friends were the Prince of Wales and Noel Coward. There is a picture of her and "Jelly Roll" posing for a photo in a sort of line dance. "Jelly Roll" was known as a pianist, composer, and talented arranger; his accomplishments are vast.

"Jelly Roll" Morton, ca. 1922 • Hogan Jazz Archive, Howard Tilton Memorial Library, Tulane University

DOMINIC "NICK" LaROCCA & THE ODJB

(b.1889, New Orleans, Louisiana - d.1961, New Orleans, Louisiana)

Nick LaRocca came out of the Irish Channel District, (locals said the river rose enough there to pick catfish out of the streets) but he was certainly not Irish; he was of Italian descent. He was the leader of the Original Dixieland Jazz Band (ODJB) when they made such a big hit in New York. The band members were called "the white guys" by the black jazz musicians, and they were certainly outnumbered there, but they took a chance and carried the sound up north to Chicago and then east to New York. The ODJB didn't seem to make a big splash in Chicago, but Al Jolson happened to hear them, and carried his well considered opinion to New York. He thought they had an exciting sound. They certainly didn't invent the sound, but when they appeared in New York, they were in the right place at the right time to catch the brass ring on the merry-go-round. They were the first jazz band to be put on celluloid.

People were not yet taking jazz music seriously and half the band members didn't take it too seriously either in the beginning, but they loved to play it. LaRocca had his own description of how jazz worked. Referring to the members of his band he said, "I cut the material, Shields puts on the lace, and Edwards sews it up" and so they presented it in New York. The rest is history and the ODJB will be famous forever in the annals of jazz remembrances.

Larry Shields played the clarinet and was really the most sensitive of all of the troupe. "Papa" Laine, who played saxaphone and sometimes drums, was a prize asset to the group because he was the most popular white musician in New Orleans. Several of the jazzmen who played brass had worked in Laine's marching and concert bands. Eddie Edwards played trombone, Henry Ragas played piano, Tony Sbarbaro (sometimes called "Spargo") played drums, and Bennie Kruger played alto sax. When they were ready to go to England, Ragas died and was replaced by J. Russell Robinson on piano. Emil Christian replaced Edwards (who did not want to go) on the trombone.

They released the world's first jazz record in 1917. It included "Livery Stable Blues" and the "Dixie Jass Band One Step" for the Victor Talking Machine Company. (Note the spelling of the word "Jass" on this first record. They still hadn't quite made up their minds on how to spell it.) Two other popular numbers were "Clarinet Marmalade" and "Tiger Rag," at first known as "No.2 Rag," which was just a hop, skip, and a jump from a French quadrille tune.

The ODJB did not improvise as much as the black bands did. In New York, Paul Whiteman and Fletcher Henderson in New York saw the appeal of the music, but didn't want to get too far into it. They mixed it with their music, which they thought would appeal to a wider audience, but it lost something. They finally learned to add more of the "black sound" to heat up the general effect.

Original Dixieland Jazz Band, L-R: Henry Ragas, Larry Shields, Eddie Edwards, Nick LaRocca, and Tony Sbarbaro, 1917. • Hogan Jazz Archive, Howard-Tilton Memorial Library, Tulane University

JOHNNY ST. CYR

(b.1890, New Orleans, Louisiana - d.1966, Los Angeles, California)

Johnny St. Cyr, ca. 1952. • Hogan Jazz Archive, Howard-Tilton Memorial Library, Tulane University

The city of New Orleans is saturated with jazz. Almost every time you turn around, you bump into someone connected in some way with jazz. Just recently I was talking to a black minister, Rev. Nathaniel Perry. He is very interested in music, from jazz to classical. He and his wife Clytie are good friends of mine. The two of them have been groundbreakers for many charitable projects in Louisiana. (Clytie developed the pilot program for Meals on Wheels in Alexandria, Louisiana.) Nat and I got to talking about jazz and he said he went to a preachers meeting in New Orleans some years back and met a lady from Grace Methodist Church whose name was St. Cyr. He said, "I don't suppose you are related to Johnny St. Cyr the great jazz banjo and guitar player," and she said "Yes, he was my husband." (Johnny had already passed on at that time.)

Johnny St. Cyr was the nerve center in Louis Armstrong's Hot Five recordings, and he played with Doc Cook's Dreamland Orchestra, on riverboats owned by the Streckfus Steamship Line in New Orleans. There use to be dances on those boats regularly. Johnny also played with Paul Barbarin and Alphonse Picou, and made a lot of recordings that are now historic.

As I have mentioned elsewhere, many of these jazz musicians had sidelines during hard times. St. Cyr's firm belief was that a good jazz musician had to be a "workin' class man." Many of the jazzmen had that same philosophy, including Louis Armstrong. When St. Cyr wasn't playing music, he was a plasterer. He said it didn't matter whether it was pickin' or plasterin', it had to be done right. Johnny St. Cyr was a plasterer. Al Rose was always good to these jazz men when they fell on hard times, and once he really needed a plasterer so he called Johnny to come and plaster a room partition which had been newly installed. He said Johnny arrived with a carton of milk to keep in the fridge and told Al he would have to get $20.00 for the job. Astonished, Al said "Twenty Dollars!" and Johnny said, "Sorry, I can't do it for less." Al said, "I thought it would be more." He gave him extra money but Johnny was a fair person and proud, so he handed the extra back. Al stayed with him while he worked to keep him company and talk with him.

Johnny was hired by Disneyland at a ripe old age to play in Los Angeles and to be their regular bandleader on the replica of the paddle wheeler *The Mark Twain*. He played there until he died.

FLETCHER HENDERSON
(b.1897, Cuthbert, Georgia - d.1952, New York)

Fletch Henderson and his Orchestra • From the Collection of The Louisiana State Museum

I must mention Fletcher Henderson briefly, because all through these narratives jazzmen left New Orleans to go play with his band at New York's Roseland. They all said it was a really tough band to play in because Henderson was a perfectionist. He was trained as a chemist before going to New York, but instead took a job as recording manager for a record company. He was also a skilled musician and found himself arranging and taking charge of the musical material that was given to him. He had an eye for talent, so he took over a band. Louis Armstrong played with him. "Jelly Roll" Morton not only played in New York, but he and Henderson shot pool together. Henderson later joined the Benny Goodman Orchestra as the first black member of an all-white orchestra.

There is a pattern in the migrations of jazzmen from New Orleans. They carried jazz all over the world, and others played it and eventually brought it back to New Orleans. Everybody always had to "come back to the well" in New Orleans, it seems, to get the "true religion" of jazz again.

PAUL BARBARIN

(b.1899, New Orleans, Louisiana - d.1969, New Orleans, Louisiana)

Paul Barbarin was a drummer who began by playing in street bands in New Orleans. He played with the Young Olympians first and became famous almost immediately. Then he went to Chicago and worked in the stockyards. Paul Barbarin would do anything he had to in order to keep on playing music. He always stayed in contact with the jazz players from New Orleans who were in Chicago. Next he played with "King" Oliver's Dixie Syncopations and with Louis Armstrong and "Jelly Roll" Morton in Luis Russell's Orchestra. Barbarin could not have had a better learning experience than that. Back in New Orleans he re-formed the famous Onward Brass Band.

Later in life he played with Sweet Emma Barrett at Preservation Hall. He played till the very end of his life and was still "in harness" when he died, leading the Onward Brass Band in a street parade. Paul Barbarin will always be fondly remembered as one of the most polite gentlemen of the jazz community.

Paul Barbarin's Band, L-R: Paul Barbarin, Arnold Metoyer, Luis Russell, Willie Santiago, and Albert Nicholas, 1919. • Hogan Jazz Archive, Howard-Tilton Memorial Library, Tulane University

LIL HARDIN ARMSTRONG

(b.1898, Memphis, Tennessee - d.1971, Chicago, Illinois)

Lil Hardin Armstrong was a brilliant pianist and vocalist. When she played in ensembles, she produced a strong rhythmic sound that seemed to hold the soul of all the band instruments together. She was the second of Louis Armstrong's four wives and probably most recognized for insisting that Louis accept the offer of Fletcher Henderson to play with his orchestra in the Roseland Ballroom. She sometimes reminisced about her years with Louis, and apparently he did too because he once said, "She was a sweet little gal but she got off the rhythm. Jazz is a workin' man's music and a workin' man's gotta play it. She didn't know nothin' about work and she got off the rhythm. She played a hell of a piano, but we was tryin' to play jazz and she got off the beat." In spite of what Louis said, she went right on as a successful pianist with various bands, and she made more recordings. She became quite famous as a club pianist all around Illinois, and eventually opened a restaurant she named the "Swing Shack."

Some musicians held a concert to memorialize Louis just two months after he died. They asked Lil to play "St. Louis Blues," and she died of a heart attack while playing it.

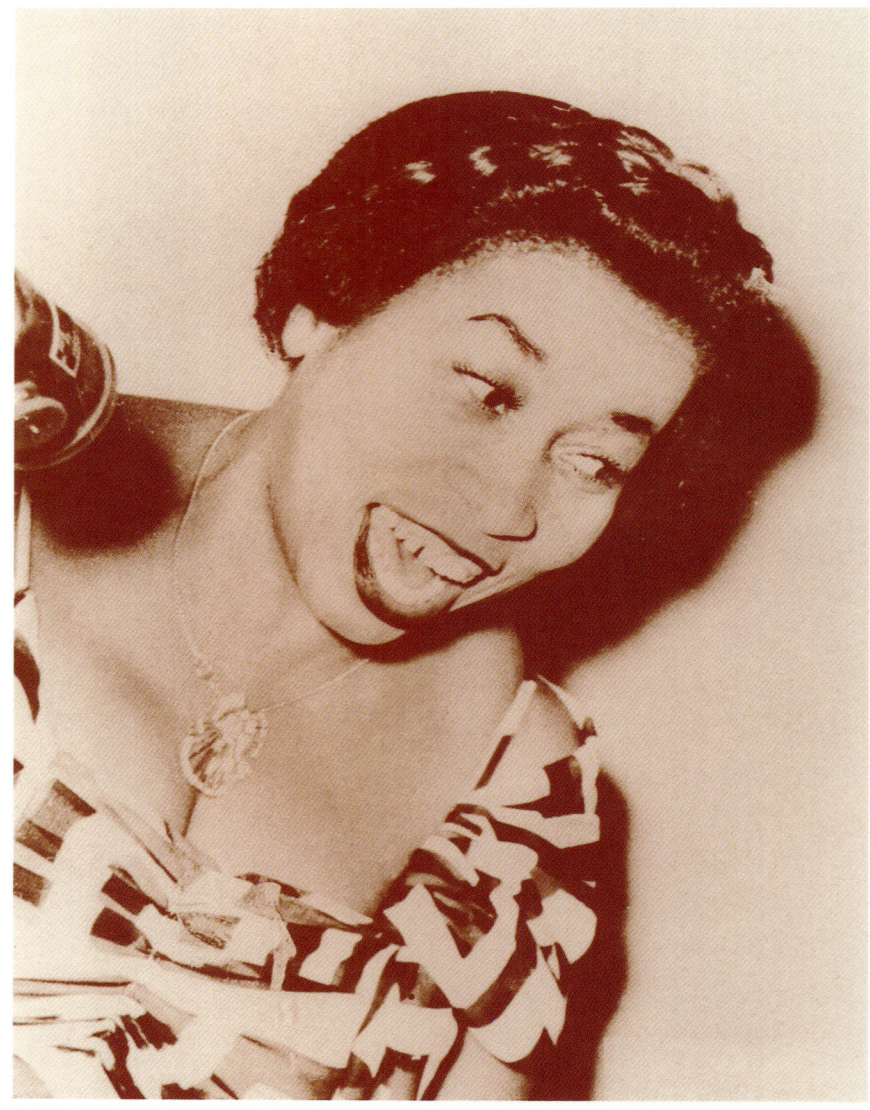

Lil Hardin Armstrong, 1954. • Courtesy The Historic New Orleans Collection, Museum/Research Center, Acc. No. 92-48-L, Fold. 2047

LOUIS ARMSTRONG

(b.1901, New Orleans, Louisiana - d.1971, New York)

Louis Armstrong is probably the most famous jazz musician that New Orleans ever produced. He grew up in the same neighborhood as Mary Fritz, a young woman who worked for my mother-in-law. It was a really rough neighborhood and they called it "the bloody bucket." Mary said people would sit on the front stoop of the house, on the banquette, on Mardi Gras morning, watching the young people in costumes, then somebody would yell "The Indians are coming!" and they would all run inside and bolt the doors.

The "Indians" were the African-American men who wore truly magnificent costumes of satin, beads and feathers. Everyone loved to see them, but by midmorning they were usually pretty well boozed up and aggressive, and the women didn't want to be around until the "Indians" had passed by. I am sure those women must have been peeking through the "jalousies" (shutters) on their doors and windows while they passed.

Knowing that background it was probably understandable that Louis got picked up for firing a revolver on New Year's Day. His grandmother was raising him and couldn't cope with that. Louis was sent to a boys home called The Waif's Home, which was the best thing that ever happened to him.

He was able to have a cornet and to get some rudimentary instruction. He once said they had first given him a bugle and there was a little hole in the horn which made him blow hard, so he was always loud.

When he finally got a cornet (from Joe "King" Oliver), he could make a really big sound. After he could make it on his own, he gave the cornet to the school so someone else could use it. Most of the jazz musicians got their start in Storyville and so did Louis. He developed a solo style which was unique, and was lucky enough to work with "King" Oliver and "Kid" Ory. He played in both their bands at different times, and finally got his own band. His most famous song became "Hello Dolly."

Louis, called "Satchmo" for his big mouth (satchel mouth), was one of the earliest jazz musicians to produce a solo recording. He literally pulled jazz out of the amateur class of street corner players and introduced a new kind of inventive, improvisational music that was unique and powerful. In addition to playing trumpet in a way few could match, he had a gravelly voice that was definitely unique. This double gift made for a winning combination that pleased audiences. He was always more of a genius than the average person realized, and he was a loveable clown.

Louis Armstrong was invited to be King Zulu one year, an integral part of Mardi Gras in New Orleans. The parade was the traditional African component of the whole celebration. We always went to see Zulu's arrival as he came in on a yacht bedecked with all the colored streamers and banners a boat could carry. Added to the decorations were many symbols of African heritage and culture. The Jahnke Company loaned them a couple of their barges, and they too were decorated for the occasion and carried the members of Zulu's court. The boats steamed up the New Basin Canal into the heart of the city.

Louis Armstrong • Hogan Jazz Archive, Howard-Tilton Memorial Library, Tulane University

LOUIS ARMSTRONG
...continued

That year the whole city went wild. Louis was the sensation of the season. We had always gone to see Zulu come in, and that year we were especially determined to see Louis as king. Zulu was always late because the party started even before the yacht and barges were boarded, but no one minded too much because the party was in high gear on the shore as well as on the water.

After the king and his court were loaded on floats, they proceeded to pay their respects to his queen, who awaited them on the balcony of the elegant Gertrude Geddes Funeral Home on Jackson Avenue. They used to throw coconuts to the crowd, and everyone wanted a Zulu coconut but too many people got hit on the head, and the city fathers finally forbade the tradition. (Now they throw Zulu doubloons.)

Louis eventually went to Chicago and worked with "King" Oliver. The duo thrilled Chicago with an interwoven stream of jazz and blues which came out of the New Orleans sound. They were recording in Chicago and their success pulled many of the jazz musicians up there. Louis eventually went on to New York.

If anyone was "Mr. Jazz", it was Louis. Even today's generation of jazz musicians believe Louis Armstrong was the most important and influential musician in the history of jazz. He liberated jazz. Many also believe it was no accidental happening in history that Louis was a musical genius. His idiosyncrasies, peccadilloes and peculiar whims only served to endear Louis to his friends. He was always proud of the pot of beans he could cook. He liked to write letters in green ink and signed them, "Red Beans and Ricely Yours, Louis." Louis became a living legend and it seemed he had discovered the fountain of youth, because he never seemed to get old. And then .... one day .... he was gone!

Louis Armstong's Hot Five (L-R: Louis Armstrong, Johnny St. Cyr, Johnny Dodds, "Kid" Ory, Lil Hardin Armstrong.) • Courtesy The Historic New Orleans Collection, Museum/Research Center, Acc No. 92-48-L, Fold. 1999

ALVIN ALCORN

(b.1912, New Orleans, Louisiana -)

Alvin Alcorn and Alphonse Picou • Hogan Jazz Archive, Howard-Tilton Memorial Library, Tulane University

Alvin Alcorn became famous as leader of the Imperial Brass Band. He went to France to represent the city of New Orleans during the United States Bicentennial and led a collection of fourteen New Orleans jazz bands in a parade down the Champs-Élysées. When Al Rose said "Can you believe that?" meaning what they had just done, Alvin answered, "We must have done somethin' right." Then he and the band flew back to Kentucky the very next day to play at the Kentucky Derby. Whenever "Papa" Celestin needed a really hot trumpet for a recording session, Alvin Alcorn was the man he sent for. He was a member of the Young Tuxedo Brass Band and the Onward Brass Band at different times, in addition to having his own band.

He never seemed to get ruffled through all the meetings with famous people and managing the bands in the street parades, and he never seemed to age. He even played a part in a James Bond movie. Alvin played with Armand J. Piron's orchestra, for "Papa" Celestin, and for Alphonse Picou, and even went out to California to replace one of "Kid" Ory's trumpeters. Ory found his perfect partner in Alcorn. Alvin's solos were outstanding, but his talent really showed in ensemble work. He could bring the sound up to a peak time after time, which really excited audiences.

DANNY BARKER and BLUE LU BARKER

Danny (b.1909, New Orleans, Louisiana - d.1994, New Orleans, Louisiana)
Blue Lu Barker (b.ca.1913, New Orleans, Louisiana - d.1997, New Orleans, Louisiana)

Danny Barker was one of the most traditional jazz musicians in New Orleans, and was truly one of New Orleans' great entertainers. He was also a fine humorist and storyteller, and he used his skills to promote and preserve traditional jazz. The jazz brass bands were Danny's favorites to watch although he himself played the guitar. He never ceased to call attention to the fact that there was a plethora of fine jazz trumpet players in New Orleans in addition to those who became famous.

Danny's wife, Blue Lu Barker, aspired to be a wonderful housekeeper, but Danny kept her busy recording with him because she was a skilled song stylist. Blue Lu developed excellent phrasing to a point where she had many imitators. She made several recordings for Decca, which were most successful. (Blue Lu passed away during the same time I was working on this book.)

Danny was Paul Barbarin's nephew. He had performed on a cigar box in a spasm band when he was a kid. Perhaps that is why he spent so much time encouraging young jazz players and teaching them what he knew. What he taught them was how to play traditional jazz. He was the all time greatest storyteller in the jazz world and that held the youngsters' attention. Leroy Jones, one of the fine young musicians in New Orleans today, and his friends used to practice in the garage, and Danny could hear them as he drove by. One day he stopped and seized the opportunity to ensure the future of New Orleans jazz. He asked them if they were interested in playing in a youth group he was forming. They definitely were, so Barker's Fairview Baptist Brass Band was born. Leroy Jones was named leader of the Fairview Band at 13. Jones says, "If it were not for Danny Barker, I probably wouldn't have gotten into traditional New Orleans jazz as early as I did."

Danny and Blue Lu Barker • Hogan Jazz Archive, Howard-Tilton Memorial Library, Tulane University

LOUIS PRIMA

(b.1911, New Orleans, Louisiana - d.1978, New Orleans, Louisiana)

Louis Prima was a precocious kid when it came to trumpets. He had an older brother, Leon, who was one of the top trumpet players in town, but Louis was playing great when he was only 12 years old. By the time he was 13 he had a band of his own, a bunch of kids. As soon as he was old enough, he was traveling the country with the band and was also doing the vocals. He would come off the stage at club dates exhausted and limp, but when he was on stage he was irrepressible. He was a headliner at the Famous Door for awhile. When he was married to Keely Smith, a saucy vocalist, they were a pretty good comedy team. Keely's special talent was to keep a straight face through all the foolishness, no matter what crazy stuff Louis came up with. George Brunies, Eddie Miller and Pee Wee Russell, all jazz regulars in New Orleans, routinely worked with his band in the 1950s. His most popular songs were, "Angelina" and "Sing, Sing, Sing." Walt Disney hired him for a role in *The Jungle Book* (as King Louie). That was pretty hysterical because he teamed up with Phil Harris and Disney got a pair of raucous voices. He was a roaring success in all the big cities – Kansas City, Las Vegas, New York and Chicago, and was always a favorite when he returned to New Orleans. He particularly liked working in Las Vegas. For awhile he had a national radio show and he appeared regularly as a guest on TV shows.

Louis Prima • Hogan Jazz Archive, Howard-Tilton Memorial Library, Tulane University

GEORGE GIRARD

(b.1930, New Orleans, Louisiana - d.1957, New Orleans, Louisiana)

George Girard was a scholar and a gentleman by all accounts. He was also a first-class trumpeter and vocalist. He and Pete Fountain played with the Basin Street Six in the 1950s. He had first gained experience playing with Phil Zito, but soon formed his own band and had great success because his trumpet style was truly exciting. Some of his music was recorded. His health began to deteriorate and he died when he was only 27 years old. It was a great loss to the New Orleans jazz community.

As I have put this book together, I have been struck by the fact that many of the jazz musicians lived to an exceptionally ripe old age, despite hard times, being up half the night, usually drinking too much, eating all the wrong things at odd hours, and generally not taking care of themselves at all. I am talking about a lot of years ago when the average life span was not nearly as long as it is now. The only reason I can think of for their many years is that they were really happy doing what they were doing, and the love of jazz must have made them feel good all the time.

George Girard's New Orleans Five, 1955. L-R: Lou Sino, Leroy Burns, Harold Cooper, Bob Discon, Bob Coquille, and Girard • Hogan Jazz Archive, Howard-Tilton Memorial Library, Tulane University

FROM THE NEIGHBORHOOD TO THE WORLD STAGE

Jazz was such a rage in New Orleans that it seemed every kid growing up, black or white, if he had any music in his soul, wanted to be in a jazz band. If enough kids in a neighborhood wanted to play and could get their hands on some musical instruments, they just naturally formed a band. If their music was any good, they could get a gig in a club somewhere or play on a street corner, and just continue to hang together. For example there was an area called Tremé Market, about where Louis Armstrong Park is now.

A whole "congregation" of potential jazzmen came out of that neighborhood – kids who had grown up together, and started their own jazz band. Alphonse Picou lived in that neighborhood. Robinson and others were from Tremé Market, including George Lewis who played clarinet; Edward Boatner who wrote "When the Saints Go Marching In"; four from the Morgan family: Sam, Isaiah, Andrew, and Albert; and a fellow called "Big Eye" Louis Nelson. Everyone resented "Jelly Roll" Morton because he was so self-important, but "Big Eye" was the one who had to admit "he come to be a real good piano player."

People asked Jim Robinson how they all got together and he said everybody was playing music when he came to town from Deer Range, Louisiana, and it was just something you had to do. These fellows all sort of hung together until they could get into one of the big bands, and most of them eventually made their own mark in the world of jazz.

There was a group that played real Dixieland who came out of the Faubourg St. John, and another came out of the Faubourg Marigny. The Faubourgs were the earliest subdivisions that were built beyond the Quarter.

There was a neighborhood in the Elysian Fields-Esplanade area that produced yet another band. The Irish Channel area was uptown,

FROM THE NEIGHBORHOOD TO THE WORLD STAGE
...continued

near the river. The channel brought together the Brunies, Nick Larocca, and others who eventually made up the components of the Original Dixieland Jazz Band.

Al Rose, as usual, was the first to notice this phenomenon of bands springing up in which all the members came out of the same neighborhood. They weren't really aware of what had happened until Al questioned some of them. Suddenly a group would produce a new and unique jazz band. One might think it would have happened in the various neighborhoods of New York, especially Harlem, but Al said it didn't seem to work like that. It was almost as if a clutch of eggs destined to produce clever chickens had been brooded and hatched in the nest of a lively neighborhood.

Louis Armstrong Park - New Orleans

A TRIBUTE TO JAZZ LOVERS

There are many people who have been protecting and promoting jazz for a lot of years. Large numbers of jazz fans in New Orleans finally got together and organized The New Orleans Jazz Club. Al Rose and Dr. Edmond Souchon were some of the movers and shakers who worked with that group, but they did much more than that.

DR. EDMOND SOUCHON

(b.1897, New Orleans, Louisiana - d.1968, New Orleans, Louisiana)

Dr. Edmond Souchon was like the guardian angel of jazz in New Orleans. He was a musician before he ever became a doctor, and he played banjo and guitar as much as his medical practice left time for. His favorite perennial joke was to tell other musicians who picked a stringed instrument, "If you pick it, it won't get well."

Souchon and Rose visited many an ailing jazz musician in his final days. They both made a great contribution to jazz and to New Orleans. Both of them were also important collectors and longtime preservationists of the history of jazz. Souchon was one who became aware that as jazz began to age a bit, it became hotter but more polished. He also noticed that "King" Oliver's band became smoother as they played at the Tulane University dances.

Souchon was a charter member of the New Orleans Jazz Club and editor of the club's publication, *Second Line*, named for the festooned marchers with fancy umbrellas who followed the marching bands. He served as club president two years. Through the efforts of many jazz lovers like Souchon, the New Orleans Jazz Festival came into being.

Dr. Edmond Souchon • From the Collection of The Louisiana State Museum

AL ROSE

(b.1916, New Orleans, Louisiana -d.1993, New Orleans, Louisiana)

Al Rose was born in New Orleans, but he followed jazz musicians all over the country. He produced close to 200 jazz concerts and put together dozens of jazz recordings under several labels. He was host of a syndicated radio program called *Journeys into Jazz*. Al authored several books and the one on Storyville was the basis for the movie *Pretty Baby*. He was very young when he started making friends with jazz musicians and through his lifetime, he became friends with hundreds of them. When Al was 22, he met "Jelly Roll" Morton. He made money for jazz musicians, helped organize bands, found jobs for musicians when they were looking for a new band, and put them to work in one of their sidelines if he couldn't find jobs for them. He was truly a colossal figure in the world of jazz because he understood the people who inhabited it. His wife, Diana, was right beside him all the way helping with all of his activities. New Orleans is deeply indebted to him for many reasons. Keeping jazz alive helped the city financially because jazz is one thing tourists come to hear. A large portion of Al's collection is now in the Jazz Archives of Howard Tilton Memorial Library at Tulane University. Al also had many other talents. He studied art with Diego Rivera, but put his art to use mostly by drawing cartoons of his friends. He was one of the world's great conversationalists and could entertain a roomful of people with his memories of funny stories, mostly about jazz musicians.

Al's father played bass and violin in the forties but he thought Al should play the flute. One day Al picked up a guitar, liked it, and began to write songs. Years later he was still helping some of the jazz musicians write lyrics.

Don Souchon and Al Rose • From the Collection of The Louisiana State Museum

JAZZ NEW ORLEANS STYLE

New Orleans musicians brought jazz together in an eclectic way. They built their music from several sources. The basis of this exciting sound definitely had a source in the drums of Congo Square mixed with the brass horns of the military. Tent shows were often set up for traveling minstrel troupes, and local musicians found out that the stringed instruments, guitars and banjos of the minstrels could be as jazzy as drums and brass horns. The local Creole musicians had been educated in the music of the clarinet and the society sound of that fine instrument brought class to jazz. New Orleans now had its own unique sound and has never lost it.

When the Army closed down Storyville during World War I, the sources of income for jazz musicians were cut in half. They had already started going to Chicago to make recordings, and Chicago was on a straight shoot from New Orleans, so it naturally followed that the jazzmen started playing in all the night clubs and restaurants in Chicago.

It was not long before musicians made the Chicago-New York connection. The ODJB had already set the scene as a foundation for jazz in New York, so the art form was in demand there and the musicians answered the call. Chicago jazz then began to set its own style to fill the vacuum. The huge market of bootleg liquor from the gangsters made the clubs flourish, and the musicians began to improvise in a new way. Some say Chicago is where New Orleans jazz is historically, because the recordings were made there, but that is not completely true. Chicago jazz became an extremely tightly organized style. It has more of a driving sound, influenced by white musicians. In some way, jazz lost its "blackness" when it moved out of New Orleans.

Memphis was a natural place for New Orleans jazz to have an influence, but it was already steeped in its native W.C. Handy's minstrel shows, and blues was heavily in control of the jazz scene. We are reminded of the "Memphis Blues" and "Beale Street Blues" to realize where their heart is.

Kansas City was another rivulet that shot off from the side of the river of jazz on its way to Chicago. The city was largely run by gangsters during the Depression years. Kansas City jazz had a heavier blues stomping sound and audiences liked a steady four beat rhythm and repetitive riffs. There was even a piece of music called "The Kansas City Stomps."

When jazz hit New York, Ferde Grofe and Paul Whiteman took hold of it and incorporated it into symphonic music. Grofe was experimenting with symphonic techniques for a jazz band and later wrote it into beautiful suites. Paul Whiteman used some of Grofe's arrangements. Whiteman's music was as classy as could be and he did use some blues sounds in it, but there wasn't too much of the pure New Orleans sound in them. His numbers were supremely elegant and he had smoothed it out so that the sound just glided up and over the room, but it was never closely related to New Orleans jazz. It is true that they took some of the raw edges off, but neither Grofe nor Whiteman was interested in improvisation.

The New Orleans musicians had always favored spots for solos in their productions, each man in turn, and so they had created an ensemble style. They had such heart and played with so much enthusiasm that they never seemed to totally relax, even when they were playing a mournful passage.

SO COME TO NEW ORLEANS AND ENJOY REAL JAZZ!

JUST A FINAL NOTE

I never cease to be amazed at the names given to jazz songs throughout the years. Most of them have to do with New Orleans or the South, but some of them really come out of left field. I just wonder how in the world any adherent to Dixieland Jazz and the blues picked a name for a song like "Tishomingo Blues." Tishomingo was an Indian Tribe way up in the northeast corner of Mississippi (there is a state park with that name there now). It was written by Spencer Williams, who also wrote one called "Shimmeshawabble" a popular song in 1915.

ORDER FORM

If you would like to order additional copies of this book or sample some of our other fine products, please fill out the form below and mail to:

YOUR POINT OF PURCHASE RETAILER
OR
R.A.L. ENTERPRISES
5749 Jefferson Highway, Harahan, LA 70123

TITLE		COST	QUANTITY	TOTAL
Jazz · New Orleans Style	64 pgs.	$8.95	_____	_____
Plantation Country Guide	64 pgs.	$8.95	_____	_____
Cookin' Country Cajun	64 pgs.	$8.95	_____	_____
Best of New Orleans Cooking	64 pgs.	$8.95	_____	_____
Favorite Recipes from New Orleans	64 pgs.	$8.95	_____	_____
Cookin' in High Cotton	64 pgs.	$8.95	_____	_____
Cookin' New Orleans Style	64 pgs.	$8.95	_____	_____
Cookin' on the Mississippi (Hard Cover)	64 pgs.	$9.95	_____	_____
Cookin' on the Mississippi (Soft Cover)	64 pgs.	$8.95	_____	_____
Best of Southern Cooking	32 pgs.	$5.95	_____	_____
Historic Houses of the Deep South	64 pgs.	$12.95	_____	_____
Mississippi River Book	128 pgs.	$10.95	_____	_____
Favorite Drinks of New Orleans	32 pgs.	$5.95	_____	_____
New Orleans	64 pgs.	$8.95	_____	_____
New Orleans on the Mississippi River	32 pgs.	$5.95	_____	_____
New Orleans - French Quarter	32 pgs.	$5.95	_____	_____
Laminated New Orleans Placemats	Set of 4	$9.95	_____	_____
Laminated Louisiana Plantation Placemats	Set of 4	$9.95	_____	_____
Laminated Mississippi Plantation Placemats	Set of 4	$9.95	_____	_____
Stationary Sets: 16 Notes, 16 Sheets & Envelopes				
Mississippi Plantations	64 pieces	$9.95	_____	_____
Louisiana Plantations	64 pieces	$9.95	_____	_____
New Orleans Jazz	64 pieces	$9.95	_____	_____
French Quarter	64 pieces	$9.95	_____	_____
Recipe Box Cards	Set of 10	$5.95	_____	_____
		Postage & Handling		$2.50
		TOTAL		_____

☐ Check Enclosed   ☐ Visa   ☐ MasterCard   ☐ American Express   ☐ Discover

Card Number _____ Expiration Date _____

Name _____

Address _____

City _____ State _____ Zip _____

Daytime Phone (_____) _____

All items are satisfaction guaranteed and your purchase will be promptly refunded if returned within 30 days.
Please allow two-four weeks for delivery. No foreign orders please.